"If you're feeling lost and brokenness has been your constant companion for way too long, this book will be the perfect gift to yourself. My friend Meshali's rich scriptural and gut-honest words paired with her gorgeous photography will renew your faith in our trustworthy God and lead your heart toward much-needed restoration. I can't wait for you to experience this beautiful book!"

Lysa TerKeurst, #1 *New York Times* bestselling author
and president of Proverbs 31 Ministries

"We all love to see the wreckage of a 'before' become the beauty of an 'after.' We impatiently watch a half-hour show, anxiously awaiting the reveal. But what if the very process is where the real beauty is revealed? In *Restored*, Meshali invites each of us to join her for a poignant journey that moves beyond a tired house into a place where our hearts find the rest of a home."

Lisa Bevere, *New York Times* bestselling author of *Without Rival*

"Meshali is a compassionate guide for anyone looking for hope and longing for home. This book is a personal but universal reminder that the deepest restoration is possible, and it will be beautiful."

Katherine Wolf, author of *Treasures in the Dark*,
Suffer Strong, and *Hope Heals*

"Meshali offers us a vulnerable picture of where our brokenness meets God's restoration. Whether you're in the midst of the fire or working toward resilience, *Restored* will meet you with practical, scriptural truth to remind you of your wholeness in Christ. The journey to healing is difficult, but this life-changing book will equip and encourage you step-by-step!"

Rebekah Lyons, bestselling author of *Rhythms of Renewal*
and *Building a Resilient Life*

"Meshali's book is a journey of renewal you will not want to miss! Much like the old wood planks in her farmhouse, the grain of our hearts is wounded in places, worn in places, and in need of being 'loved back to life.' With the familiar creak of a Southern porch door, Meshali tenderly and bravely welcomes us into the renovation of her farmhouse, even as she shares the restoration of her heart, the healing of wounds from trauma, and the hope that God will indeed do the same in us."

Elisabeth Hasselbeck, Emmy Award–winning television host and *New York Times* bestselling author

"The only time I put this book down was to take notes and answer the thoughtful questions Meshali offers at the end of each chapter. With beauty and tenderness, she welcomes you into her story of renovation and restoration. You can't help but feel comfortable enough to share your own!"

Lauren Chandler, author, worship leader, songwriter

"The words in *Restored* are transformative. Meshali invites us to take a front-row seat to her story and so graciously reveals that restoration doesn't happen overnight. Her profound outlook provides us with spiritual and personal insight, and practical training wheels for our own journey. Line by line, we see the power of the process unfold. While we are in a hurry, the God of process is not. This book demands a new perspective and pushes the reader to hope again!"

Taylor Madu, co-pastor, Social Dallas Church

"Meshali is so incredibly warm and generous with her life and her story, I honestly couldn't put this book down! I don't know if I've ever experienced a more loving and compelling invitation into what it looks like to actively abide in the heart of God. *Restored* offers the reader some truly beautiful, hands-on tools and spiritual practices to help us partner with the Lord as he's making all things new in our hearts and lives!"

Christy Nockels, singer-songwriter, podcaster, author of *The Life You Long For: Learning to Live from a Heart of Rest*

"Sometimes we need to see physical restoration to have our eyes opened to the God who restores. Meshali gives us that restoration tour in this book. From reviving her floors to installing new wallpaper and pipes,

Meshali invites us into more than just a tale of home restoration. In these pages, she invites us into the arms of God."

Sara Hagerty, bestselling author of *Unseen: The Gift of Being Hidden in a World That Loves to Be Noticed*, *Every Bitter Thing Is Sweet*, and *The Gift of Limitations*

"Like many others, I first came across Meshali Mitchell through her stunning photographs. In *Restored*, we are now introduced to her breathtaking gift of storytelling. From the very first chapter, I was drawn in and moved by the kindness of God to bring about change. With transparency, warmth, hope, and a whole lot of heart, Meshali reminds us that when we fall, he picks us up. That when we can't see a way, he makes a way. And most of all, that Jesus is our restorer. Her message is one the world desperately needs. This book will inspire and help so many people."

Beth Redman, songwriter, speaker

RESTORED

RESTORED

PARTNERING WITH GOD IN TRANSFORMING OUR BROKEN PLACES

Meshali Mitchell

Revell

a division of Baker Publishing Group
Grand Rapids, Michigan

Published by Revell
a division of Baker Publishing Group
Grand Rapids, Michigan
RevellBooks.com

Printed in China

Library of Congress Cataloging-in-Publication Data
Names: Mitchell, Meshali, author.
Title: Restored : partnering with God in transforming our broken places / Meshali Mitchell.
Description: Grand Rapids, Michigan : Revell, a division of Baker Publishing Group, 2025. | Includes bibliographical references.
Identifiers: LCCN 2024034033 | ISBN 9780800746209 (cloth) | ISBN 9781493448579 (ebook)
Subjects: LCSH: Spiritual healing—Religious aspects—Christianity. | Psychic trauma—Religious aspects—Christianity. | Repairing—Social aspects.
Classification: LCC BT732.5 .M574 2025 | DDC 234/.131—dc23/eng/20240805
LC record available at https://lccn.loc.gov/2024034033

Cover illustration by Nate Eidenberger

Interior book design by Nadine Rewa

Published in association with Yates & Yates, www.yates2.com.

Baker Publishing Group publications use paper produced from sustainable forestry practices and postconsumer waste whenever possible.

25 26 27 28 29 30 31   7 6 5 4 3 2 1

To my amazing family whom I
love and cherish so deeply.

And to everyone who
needs the restoration
only Jesus offers.

CONTENTS

FOREWORD

I love Meshali, so I opened this beautiful book for the first time with a wide smile and high expectations. I wasn't at all surprised to find it rife with biblically sound truisms, but this one observation startled me:

"He has leveled the ruins of my life and erected beauty in its place."

When I read that sentence, I paused, put the book down, and walked over to my desk to get a highlighter because I wanted to remember it. Frankly, if I weren't a conservative, sixty-year-old Bible teacher living in the Deep South, I'd be sorely tempted to tattoo it somewhere on myself because I think it's such a profound synopsis of the gospel of Jesus Christ. And while the concept of restoration is all too familiar in Christian culture as we proclaim it from pulpits and embed it in our song lyrics, we Christ followers in the developed world tend to conveniently forget that something *must* be broken—effectively ruined—before restoration can take place.

When I first brought my daughter, Missy, home from Haiti after an arduous adoption journey, I assumed we'd navigated the hardest part of our story. Mind you, I'd read an entire shelf full of books about what to expect when expecting and had spent most of my discretionary "shoe money" on counseling with a therapist specializing in international adoptions, but I still wasn't prepared for all the emotional intricacies of parenthood. Because someone else's opinion can't fully prepare you for your child's first projectile food poisoning experience after enthusiastically ingesting a bowlful of bad shrimp! Nor can someone else's empathy hold your baby girl while she sobs over her first mother's death. Navigating the unexpected and processing pain are uniquely personal experiences.

Plus, pain is relative. Your child might suffer with the effects of the flu for a few days, or your child might suffer with a debilitating disease for the rest of their life. You might have a fight with your spouse that leaves your heart bruised, or you might go through a divorce that leaves your heart battered. Some people lose their jobs as the result of downsizing, and some people lose their breasts as the result of cancer. Some hardships leave faint scars on our psyches while others leave jagged fissures that slice all the way to the marrow of our souls. Yes, pain is relative, but it's unavoidable.

No one gets through this life unscathed, y'all. Every single one of us will deal with pain and suffering at some level, and any grown-up who insists they haven't is either lying, mentally disturbed, or has amnesia! Now, before you hurl this book—this harvest of all the blood, sweat, and tears Meshali has sowed—across the room because you picked it up thinking it was about restoration and *not* depression, here's the good news:

God's compassion and glory are often highlighted in the milieu of human hardship.

Remember the thirty-three Chilean miners who were trapped underground for sixty-nine days in 2010? An estimated one *billion* people watched the dramatic live television coverage of their rescue. Yet, weeks prior to their heartwarming rescue, when their fate looked to be sealed over two thousand feet below the surface, nineteen-year-old miner Jimmy Sanchez sent a letter via a drilled air vent to the surface that read, in part, "There are actually thirty-four of us down here because God has never left us."[1] And Jose Henriquez, who functioned as a lay

14

pastor to his trapped crewmates, later expounded on God's palpable presence: "God didn't need any doors to get down there in the middle of the mine where we were. Every time we called on His name, He came. He was there, and He was present."[2]

Henriquez described how one week before they were rescued, he held a worship service and preached the gospel to his friends. When his fellow miners—who'd become like brothers during their grueling, two-month ordeal—were presented with this opportunity to dedicate their lives to Jesus Christ, twenty-two of them professed their faith in him. The very last thing the thirty-three did before ascending to safety was to gather around the rescue capsule and pray, praising God for saving their lives. Henriquez now refers to the sixty-nine days they spent trapped in the mine as "God's accident" because he believes God used it to make himself known.

The honest awareness of our own brokenness, coupled with the cognizance that self-rescue isn't an option, is a necessary catalyst for spiritual rescue and restoration. Sadness is not the opposite of hope, it's the smoke signals our broken hearts send up for help . . . the rocks our souls painstakingly drag to the beach to spell out S-O-S when we feel stranded on the island of suffering. Sorrow proves that while we may be running on mere fumes of faith, we're still in the race. In the context of Christian faith, our disappointment, disillusionment, and even despair can be emotional indicators that we believe we were made for more and that somehow, some way, God will come to our aid and redeem what's gone crazy wrong in our little corner of the world. Anguish is not the opposite of hope—apathy is.

I believe our Creator Redeemer will use Meshali's story as a healing balm in your own. But I also pray you'll pick up the proverbial sword the following pages unsheathe because it's powerful enough to kill hope-stealing dragons.

Warmest regards,
Lisa Harper

PART 1

RUIN

1

PARADISE LOST

You Are Worthy of Restoration

I'm standing outside a charming, falling-down farmhouse, where two tall pine trees seem to stand guard over me in the front yard. I love pine trees and the tone of their green. Slowly, I walk the perimeter. This house has been on the market for a good while, tucked away from the road on a pretty little piece of land right in the heart of a suburban setting. The best of both worlds. But many potential buyers have passed on it due to its age and its worn and weathered state.

For a while now I've had a yearning in my heart to settle down and plant deep roots. I've been living in downtown Dallas in a one-bedroom loft, living life on the go, running a growing, thriving photography business.

On a recent Sunday at church, I stopped Meredith, a realtor friend of mine, in the lobby as we were leaving.

"Hey," I told her, "I think I'm ready to purchase my first home."

The words escaped my mouth sooner than I had expected, surprising me on their way out. I knew the yearning was there, but was I actually ready for this big step? How does anyone really know when they're ready for a commitment like this?

Meredith so kindly agreed to help me. Over the next several weeks she and I set out to look at a few contenders, but none of them were right for one reason or another.

Then, she called me one night while I was in Nashville.

"Okay, don't hang up," she said. "I found a house that I want you to see. It's an old farmhouse that might be just right for you, but it will need some work, definitely some TLC."

As she proceeded to tell me about the property, my heart was drawn to it. This little farmhouse had been built and cherished by the same family since 1886, but through the years it had become a bit run-down. The house just needed the right person with the right eye to love it back to life, Meredith told me.

The idea captured my imagination and went wild. But another part of me told me to run and run hard—in the other direction.

Awhile later, Meredith FaceTimed me and walked the property and house. I could see the potential, but I just wasn't sure I could take on such a big project. I didn't know a thing about home restoration. That was the stuff for the professionals, like the HGTV people—not me.

But the house wouldn't let me go. After a few days of thought and prayer, I returned to Dallas–Fort Worth and decided to visit the property myself.

So here I am. As I step onto the property, I feel the mystery of joy and a tingle of hope coursing through my body while I stare at mostly ruins before me. Circling the farmhouse, I see a lot of the wood siding is rotting out. I run my fingers over the surface and a piece crumbles into my hand. Somehow, this doesn't alarm me one bit. I step up onto the porch that spans the front of the house and notice the old porch swing. Suddenly I see my bare feet stretching past my denim pants, pushing off the porch boards while I rock back and forth. I envision my friends and loved ones swinging with me and all the stories we'll share between us.

As I step inside through the front door, golden light cascades across the dark wooden floors. These dear planks have seen a lot of life, and I see beauty in the spots where the finish has worn off.

I breathe it all in. It smells like an old house—like that curiously universal smell of a grandparent's home. I work my way into the entryway and begin to look around. Moving room to room, I snap in and out of reality as the weight of my feet creates loud creaks that echo through a home with a nearly endless list of things in need of repair, while I also dream of what the rooms will look like if we gut, paint, and furnish them into new life. I see hope and life here, beyond what is. This house is full of soul, full of stories. There's a whole lot more than old ruins here. I see beauty.

In my mind's eye, I see this house in its future state, sitting there on the hill in all its glory—loved, restored, made new.

Even better than new.

Deep down, I can't deny the truth: It's almost like the house is calling out to me. And I have this longing to love something back to life.

My own life had needed reviving long before I ever saw the farmhouse or thought about taking on a restoration project. Isn't that often how these metaphors in life go, these ways God teaches us through a process of one thing or another? This house began a process for me that only God could have orchestrated. This book is no memoir; it's not my story but ours. It's a space of refuge—a spot on my porch I invite you to share with me. You see, the newness of loving something back to life begins with story—the stories you and I bring to the table, the ones that sometimes have hard beginnings and middles . . . and the Greater Story that changes the lens of our reading and writes our ending.

As we journey through this book together and find the inroads to discovering restoration in *your* story, we'll start with some small pieces of mine.

I experienced my childhood as a time of security and freedom, years when I was free to be a kid. Looking back now, those carefree years seem so brief.

I grew up in a little town in Arkansas, the oldest child in a preacher's family. When I was two weeks old, my dad felt the call to preach and began to travel all over the nation, holding revival services. This made for a unique ministry family model because he wasn't the pastor of a single church but was in full-time service to the larger body of Christ. To this day my dad is an evangelist, traveling and preaching forty-eight weeks a year or more.

That's all I've ever known.

As our family grew and my brother and sister were born, my dad traveled, Mom stayed home with us, and we continued our family roots in our hometown. My grandparents from both sides lived there. In my young mind, I couldn't have imagined a more picture-perfect family. We might have been a bit disconnected, but we were together. To this day I don't recall much heavy hardship in those early years. In my little mind, we were "livin' the dream," with pretty houses and nice cars, friends we loved, and a great school.

Occasionally, but rarely, I got to travel with my dad, staying in hotels and seeing new places. He ministered and preached in a lot of rural churches around America—some bigger, some tiny.

When I was around nine years old, I attended a revival meeting with him in Missouri. As the revival meeting that evening was approaching, he said, "Meshali, let's go early and pray before the service tonight for the people coming." We went to the empty sanctuary an hour before service time, I put my little hand in his, and we walked the aisles of that empty room. We walked together and prayed for the people that would soon sit in those seats. I had my head down, but my eyes were squinting as I watched Dad's black dress shoes walk the old floors, saw him place his other hand on the edge of each wooden pew. I could hear his voice every few steps, asking the Lord to touch hungry hearts. I remember a particular cedar smell in my dad's suit jacket, the oil on the pews, and how our feet felt walking on that church carpet.

As we walked that sanctuary, even as a kid I knew there was something holy and sacred about doing the unseen work—the work of service to people. I wanted to help people when I grew up. The feeling of loving and ministering to others made me come alive too. Just like Dad.

I also had a passion for all things creative. That I definitely got from my mom. She always had a gift for making things pretty. The Lord had wired me with empathy, compassion, and an artist's eye. From an early age, it's like I could feel and sense things others maybe couldn't or didn't look for. At the time I didn't know exactly what any of that meant, but even then I knew Jesus's teaching: "Do you love me? . . . Feed my sheep" (John 21:17). He was already cultivating something in me. I was sure the

Lord had placed these passions within me—helping to encourage people, teaching, working with the arts. All of it somehow merged inside of me.

That young season of life was full and busy. It was school and sports and church and family. I'd come running in our house after school with a flushed face and wide grin, grabbing snacks and jumping on my bike alongside my brother and sister. Our bikes crunched over the trails through the long piney woods of south Arkansas with every spare second we had. It was either bikes or four-wheelers for us. We would stuff our backpacks full of Doritos and Dr Pepper, get on our Huffy ten-speeds, and ride the hills of our neighborhood until dark.

There was a huge steep hill beside our house at the edge of the woods, and I would build speed and coast down it, holding my legs out as far as they could go, feeling the wind blow my curly blond hair. I breathed it all in—the laughter, the leaning side to side as we sped. My brother and sister would follow, and we would talk and ride till sunset, stopping here and there and building forts that no other kids in the neighborhood could dare to rival. We never drifted too far away from home, always safe and sure on those trails in our small, quaint neighborhood. We just had to make it home before the sun set.

All week we were home with Mom, and on Thursdays Dad came home from preaching out on the road. Every summer both sides of our family frequented the banks of stunning Arkansas lakes. We knew the ways of the water almost before we knew how to walk. Summer mornings in the pines, I woke up to the sound of water lapping the bank outside the window of our camper and the scents of bacon and coffee filling the air. My grandparents, parents, aunts and uncles, siblings and cousins were all there. After long days on the water, we would sit around the bonfire and talk into the night. Some in my family fished in the early morning hours, and then we would sit around and talk some more. I was always the observant kid who spent time listening to the adults and soaking it in. Mom and my grandmothers cooked, and we kids played at the campsites. Our carefree getaways ended with sunburnt faces, laughter, and the best memories. I sure collected them, and I remember and savor them now.

One night toward sunset, when I was around six years old, we got in the ski boat and went out on the glass-smooth lake. Dad got in the water with me and yelled to everyone, "I'm gonna teach her to ski today." He was so confident I could do it. He whispered to me, "I'm gonna hold you and make sure you're steady, and when the boat takes off, just hold the rope and just stand on the ski. All you gotta do is stand." I heard the boat start and my heart pounded. The engine revved a couple times, and before I knew it I was gliding on top of the water, just like Dad said. Everyone in the boat rose to their feet cheering, and I swelled with joy. I come from a family of athletes and water skiers (and overachievers), so this was something to celebrate. My little heart was beaming from the moment I stood up on that water to when I laid my head down to sleep that night. Those were the feelings and the memories that would sustain me for years.

Because the next six years were full of the complexities life hands us all. Life with unmet needs. Life with pain intertwined even with the good memories.

And then in what felt like a sudden moment but wasn't, all of that childhood freedom and promise slipped through my fingers.

The first time trauma came to visit me was when I was twelve years old. I felt like it came into my life abruptly and brought its cousins—fear, depression, and worry—along with it. For years after, I had battles with this wounding. It would douse me in physical, emotional, and relational ways, like pouring buckets of rain over my head again and again. This pain came despite my being born into a God-fearing family and knowing Jesus from a young age. Of course, faith doesn't spare anyone from trouble, but these rains seemed to soak through my sense of self-esteem and the way I believed God thought about me.

During this time, my parents went through a divorce that was really hard on all of us. The life I had loved so much seemed to end with a cataclysmic crash. I experienced the deep pain of a broken home and other traumas that deeply impacted me in my developmental years. I was so young, so immersed in it, that I had no ability to pull back and gain any true perspective on the pain. As adults, we have the gift of a 30,000-foot view on life and are able to see how divorce's blow affects everyone involved—kids, parents, every person it touches. It causes a lot of pain for everyone involved, and it's not just a one-time event but more like a nuclear bomb as we deal with the fallout and consequences time and time again. Depression, anxiety, loneliness, shame, and worry became my constant companions.

As the years passed, our family was attempting to put the pieces together again. My stepmom and stepsister joined our hearts and lives during this time. We were a blended family all growing together, each of us doing the very best we could with what we'd been given. Life continued on in this new form, and we all were working to rebuild. But my heart was hurting. Now I look back and see the Lord was expanding and adding to our family even in the midst of pain, but at the time it was hard for me to heal and grow in health because of the brokenness I was experiencing and had not yet dealt with.

Joy felt hard to find.

If there is one remarkably clear aspect of my journey toward restoration, it is the hope I found as God proved his faithfulness to me again and again. If past pain and heartache is also familiar to you—whether similar to mine or radically different—I want you to have that hope as soon as possible, because God wants to minister healing and restoration to you too.

Before I fully experienced God's tender care, I spent a long time feeling stuck. At some point in my young life I decided this as fact: I could never fully heal or recover from all of the pain. The girl who woke with no worries and coasted down hills and slept easy felt like a distant memory. Instead, I was a kid carrying weights too heavy for my shoulders, burdens I was never built for.

As tragic as that belief was for me, I also decided it wasn't a big deal to God. Perhaps like some of you reading this book, I felt God could not be bothered with my problems. Though I suspected he *could*, I was not convinced he *would* make a way for me to have the abundant life Jesus

promised in John 10:10 to those who love him. Abundance wouldn't be my lot in life. Healing may be available to others, but my problems were too complex, and it was way out of my reach. Impossible.

By the time I was a young adult, I had filed away long lists of seemingly impossible things deep in the hidden places of my heart. I made agreements with myself to just live with all the hardships, losses, and grief.

If I'm honest, I believed in the pain more than I believed in God's promises.

I look back on those years of my life as a season of deep, abiding grief, even when the waters stilled. Grief is pain attached to a loss. We often think of grief in terms of the death of a loved one, but grief comes with thousands of little "deaths": the end of a career, of a relationship, of a dream, of innocence.

God's love pours hope over the ashes of our lives.

The tangible pain of grief makes its way into our bones, shape-shifting in more ways than we can often perceive in the moment. Not all grief looks the same, and how we grieve is unique to each of us. But all expressions of grief reflect deep sorrow, and this is a normal part of life. Even Jesus was "a man of sorrows and acquainted with grief" (Isa. 53:3).

Sometimes grief slips into despair. Despair says, "I have lost everything, and it can never be restored." Despair clutched me too, but the grace of God always rescued me from its grip. Our grief doesn't have to look like the grief of someone who doesn't know God. The apostle Paul spoke to this when he wrote that believers in Christ can grieve *with hope* (see 1 Thess. 4:13–18).

In fact, sometimes hope is exactly what comes of our losses. God's love pours hope over the ashes of our lives. Romans 5:3–5 says, "We rejoice in our sufferings, knowing that suffering produces endurance, and endurance produces character, and character produces hope, and hope does not put us to shame, because God's love has been poured into our hearts through the Holy Spirit who has been given to us." When we are right in the middle of grief and the thought of rejoicing is far from our reach, this encouragement may be hard to feel. But *it is true.*

As Christ followers, we live in an upside-down kingdom. We can rejoice not only in future glory but in our present trials and sufferings. Even here in this dark place of grief there is something beautiful being produced in us. It's in this place that a *transformation of heart* is happening as we are partnering with God in his story for us.

About fifteen years ago, I decided to face the pain as best I knew how and saw a counselor for the first time. I pulled into the parking lot of the little church where she had an office and realized I felt woozy and weak. The walk from my car to the side door felt a mile long. The thought of walking in and opening up my life, of telling someone about my journey and some of the road I had walked, made my palms sweat and my knees feel like they might buckle. My face felt hot and numb. Taking this huge step of trusting another person with certain areas of my heart felt risky for me.

Peggy met me in the hallway, and her kind eyes and sweet smile immediately settled my heart a bit.

"Ah, you must be Meshali. I'm so happy to meet you."

Her voice was gentle but steady and sure, which helped slow my heart rate and allowed me to take a deep breath. She welcomed me into her office, and we sat across from each other at a little wooden table with a box of Kleenex that I was sure I would need. I remember saying, "I don't really know how to do this." I've long suffered from perfectionism—and even in counseling I couldn't kick it.

Peggy's questions felt like keys to unlock the secret places of my heart. Our first sessions felt like testing waters, stepping out from dry land into the shallows. Then we waded deeper into the dark blue waters where it was harder to see what was below me. During one specific session, a dam seemed to break. Hot tears streamed down my face as I began to open up, answering her questions without holding back and sharing some of the things I'd buried for so long. As we excavated the ruins, I felt an unbearable heaviness lifting off my shoulders. I put my forehead on the desk and watched my tears drip over the wood and down onto my jeans.

After this release, hope began to seep through the door of my heart. It had been so long since that kind of hope—restorative hope—had visited me. When I looked back up, I saw love and compassion in Peggy's eyes—the opposite of the picture my anxiety had painted.

She said, "Meshali, the Holy Spirit is going to do a beautiful healing work in your life. It will be a bit like heart surgery. It's going to be messy, take time, and involve some pain in recovery. But he is going to heal you fully. The truth is going to set you free. Are you ready?"

I had never felt so hopeful. I felt loved, seen, known. I nodded and replied with a weak but sincere voice. "Yes, I am."

I was ready to see clearly.

For many years now, God has been working a miracle in my life. A miracle of restoration.

In this age of HGTV and DIY and home-improvement celebrities, we might think of *restoration* as a synonym for *renovation*—an improvement that results in something fresher, more functional, more valuable, more Instagram-worthy. Really great renovations become trends like barn doors and outdoor kitchens. And okay, a renovated life might be a prettier life. But the kind of restoration I'm talking about gets at something much more important than appearances.

When God made us, he gave us an identity. We know this as the *imago Dei*, the image of God in us (Gen. 1:27). God created us to bear his likeness, but this fallen world has distorted what that looks like. Jesus came to restore us to the Father's original intention for humanity, to redeem our brokenness, set us back in our rightful place as sons and daughters of God, and make everything new. His life, death, and resurrection are for all of us collectively and individually. Through Jesus we can be restored to God's specific purpose for our life.

Before trauma came into my life, I had a glimpse of what my life could be: joyful, creative, connected, purposeful. That particular vision vanished for years until I invited the Lord to undertake his restoration of my mind, body, and spirit. I finally believed that he not only *could* do it . . . but that he *would*.

I'll be done restoring my farmhouse before he's finished with me, I'm sure.

While walking this journey of restoration in both my heart and home, the Lord has used some of my greatest pain to reveal himself to me. After great suffering, Job said to God, "My ears had heard of you but now my eyes have seen you" (Job 42:5 NIV). As I was raised in church and in a ministry family, for many years my ears heard of the Lord. But through my restoration, I feel like my eyes have now seen the Lord in new ways and my heart truly knows him! He sustains me when I need strength, comforts me when I need true comfort, and gives me hope when I don't know if I can make it through the day.

None of us can avoid pain in this broken world, but what we do with it and who we take it to matters. My true life began only when I partnered with God in my healing. Then I began to see real transformation.

God isn't loving who you used to be, or even a future version of who you long to be, but he is loving who you are, as you are, right where you are . . . today.

Something tells me if you are holding this book you may be hurting right now, and if you are, I am so sorry. I know things may look bleak and the pain you are enduring can feel simply unbearable at times. I just want to sit right here with you for a second and love you. Know this: God sees you right where you are this day, and he loves you. He isn't loving who you used to be, or even a future version of who you long to be, but he is loving who you are, as you are, right where you are . . . today. Soak in this truth and ask the Lord to help you receive it. This assurance of his love is foundational to your healing.

Brokenness is so hard to endure that sometimes we hold the pieces and don't even know how to begin to put them back together. God is working on your behalf, even when all you can do is stand still in the shattered fragments of your life. Scripture promises that he will comfort us in every trial and sorrow (2 Cor. 1:3–4) and that he will complete the work he started in us (Phil. 1:6). This fallen world brings us many trials, many sorrows, but Jesus has promised to be with us through it all as we move toward our eternal home, where everything will be perfect, without sorrow or pain (Rev. 21:4).

This is the journey I'd like to take with you—through grief toward healing and wholeness. The fact you're reading this means you desire and have faith for restoration. The good news is that even if your faith is just the size of a mustard seed, that's all you need. I once believed that abundance wasn't my lot in life, but I don't believe that anymore. And if you've ever held that thought to be true in your own life, I pray you don't believe it anymore either.

I wish I could sit right there with you in person. I'd slide my chair right up to you, knee to knee, and look right into your eyes and tell you *restoration is possible for you through Christ* no matter what your pain looks like. Even as I'm typing this, I feel the compassion of Christ over you and over whatever situation you're facing. I feel hope in my bones now as I prayerfully encourage you. I stand with you in the promise that he is with us through every part of this journey through the valley of the shadow of death and out into light, life, and love.

In the run-down farmhouse kitchen, paper peels off the walls, water stains mark the ceiling, and the faint scent of mouse droppings hits me. I stand in the tiny space and turn in a full circle, taking it all in. None of this is my responsibility yet. Do I really want to take on a project like this?

I stand here and my imagination flashes from scene to scene. I wonder about the people who made coffee here, cooked meals here, ate at the table and washed dishes in the sink. What were their joys and dreams? What did they suffer? If the house has a story to tell, it's something about the hardships of life having more strength than we do to stay above them. I know a thing or two about that. The home's potential calls out to me beyond the brokenness.

My plan to put down roots never looked like this in my mind, in my daydreams. Signing the papers to buy this home will be a big undertaking for me. Restoring it will be a slow and thorough process if I'm to do it right. It will require learning. It will require experts. It will require time and money I'm not sure I have. It will ask nothing less of me than my constant devotion.

Thoughts run through my head, things others have said to me:

I'm sure it was a pretty place at one time, but that's too big an undertaking.

Meshali, do you really understand the amount of work and commitment that would go into buying a place like that?

You have other things on your plate. You don't want to take on a project like that with all you have going on.

I hear them loud and clear. But my wounded and sluggish soul needs this for reasons I can't completely explain. As I turn in my tight, tiny circle, I see this room for what it might be instead: bright, warm, clean, filled with the scents of a home-cooked meal. I have a vision for this space that I can't unsee.

I have lived too long in a world limited by how I feel or what I can see with my eyes.

With vision we see what is possible, for worse or better. Vision—seeing not just what is but what could be—is a powerful skill. My vision for that kitchen, for this itty-bitty run-down farmhouse, is restoration. Not just a return to some trendy appearance of newness, but a return to its original intention and function. Not just a kitchen, but a place of nourishment. Not just a house, but a home. I see this home as it was created to be before things deteriorated: clean and whole, fortified against the elements, safe and warm and pleasant inside. Welcoming . . . for people. I see life in this home: friends gathered around the table laughing, little feet scampering across the floor, maybe even my future family.

I see all the beauty that can be.

And it's going to take a miracle.

I call Meredith and tell her yes. This house is the one for me.

RESTORATION PRACTICE

Grieve Your Losses by Writing a Lament

What sorrow are you facing? God invites you to tell him all about it, especially if you feel he has abandoned you. If you're not sure what to say, use the prompts in the following list, which is adapted from a framework for writing a lament offered by Christian scholar Graham Joseph Hill.[1] Take as much time as you need with each element, giving yourself permission to pour out your honest, deepest, unsanitized emotions to the Lord.

1. *Cry out*: Address God directly.
2. *Complain*: Let it all out—your anger, pain, heartache, or sadness.
3. *Remember*: Recall God's presence in your past or the evidence of God's power you have witnessed in the lives of others.
4. *Request*: State your deepest desire.
5. *Argue*: Make your case for why God should intervene.
6. *Rage*: Accuse your enemies before God.
7. *Trust*: State your confidence that God hears you.
8. *Promise*: Express your desire to offer praise to God.
9. *Thank*: Appreciate whichever attribute of God you are thankful for in the moment.

2

EVERY
HEART
BUT MINE

Your Restoration Is Never Beyond Repair

Meredith and I are standing in the dusty, empty living room, taking in the warped floorboards (are they safe to walk on?), ancient light fixtures (electrical fire hazards, to be sure), and mildew creeping down the walls (time will tell where the plumbing problems are). None of this bothers me. I envision gorgeous hardwood, fresh fixtures, and clean, textured walls.

Almost without thinking I say, "If I could just gut this place, I could start with a blank slate and go from there!"

Even with my nonexistent home restoration experience, I understand a fundamental truth about it: Not everything that's broken can be repaired. Much of it has to be thrown out, not for careless or cosmetic reasons but for practical matters of safety and cost, not to mention building codes. Before I can add anything new to this house, I have to get rid of anything old that no longer serves it, anything that might make it unsafe to live in. It will do me no good to buy furniture and rugs that will only fall through the floor or to have mold growing through layers of paint. I have to expose anything that might lead to future problems. I have to unearth everything unseen, examine it, assess it, and decide on the wisest course of action. Before I paint and make it pretty, I need to make sure the bones are good.

"Let's gut it," I say again. "Let's rip it back to the studs and rebuild from there."

Meredith sees it with me, more friend than realtor. She and I have had what feels like hundreds of phone calls during this season, her assuring me and cheering me on that God is in this decision and is with me in this new adventure. Something about her reassurance and presence makes restoration seem all the more possible.

During the years of my traumas and their aftermath, I often felt I had been gutted against my will. In the years of my healing, I had to do some voluntary gutting, identifying the things in my life that were causing more harm than good.

Chief among them were some of my thought patterns.

Being in a ministry family isn't always easy, and as a young person I often felt fully exposed, like I was struggling alone in a glass house where every outsider could see me. I learned to push things down and hide behind a mask of perfectionism. In fact, the more I pressed down, the more my need to perform and be perfect raised its head. The standard I set for myself was oftentimes off-the-charts unattainable. I excelled in school, at church, and in sports. I didn't approach *anything* with a lighthearted mindset, constantly trying to validate my worth like my identity depended on it.

If I'm not perfect, I'm not worth it.

I received awards, acceptance, and applause from others that I'd hoped would eventually mend my internal wounds. But the more accolades I got, the more I had to fight to keep them—and the truest, most authentic parts of myself felt unknown and unseen.

Don't you people know I'm exhausting myself to keep this up?

The hamster wheel of performance created only exhaustion, depression, and more grief. The enemy came to steal, kill, and destroy (John 10:10), and he seemed to be wreaking havoc on my life, my heart, and my relationship with God. My lament felt a lot like Mary's after Lazarus died. She never doubted God's power, only his willingness to help. "Lord," she accused Jesus when he showed up several days after Lazarus's burial, "if you had been here, my brother would not have died" (John 11:21).

Lord, if you had been there, these terrible things would not have happened.

Lord, if you had just shown up on time, these terrible things would not have happened to me.

Lord, why aren't you delivering me from this torment in my head? Even now, after all this, why aren't you showing up for me?

Jesus showed his power by raising Lazarus from the dead. But in my world, as year of suffering followed year of suffering, I began to doubt I was worthy of that kind of miracle.

I carried these troubles through my teens and into college. I felt stuck, like maybe depression and these holes in my heart would simply be my lot in life. Had God dealt me a bad hand?

Many of us, having lost precious dreams, relationships, opportunities, ideals, beliefs, and so on, get busy figuring out what it's going to take to get them back. How much energy will heal me? How much money, how much work, how much belief? Would God finally heal me then?

By the time I was in my midtwenties, the futility of these efforts stared me in the face.

When grit and elbow grease don't get us where we want to be, some of us decide we'll just stay where we are physically, mentally, and spiritually. We can't see a way to overcome the disrepair. We don't have enough resources or know-how. Even in desperate need of repair, staying where we are is at least familiar. I'm not exactly sure how my heart got so stuck in that place of futility, but I couldn't seem to work myself out of it. I was trying so hard—by my own efforts—and I was failing. It felt like I was putting Band-Aids over bullet holes and bleeding out in my emotions, thoughts, and relationships.

Then thoughts about why this was happening turned on me.

I started battling vicious thought cycles that felt as if they were taking me under. For a long time, I heard the soundtrack of what I call a "trauma narrative" rooted in shame playing on a loop in my head. It sounded like this:

God can help everyone, but my issues are too big and too deep. I'm the exception.

God doesn't care for me. If he did, I wouldn't be stuck in this mental and emotional anguish.

God is not pleased with me. He stays upset with me.
I have to produce and perform and be the best to really have value.
I will always be alone.
I will never come back from this.
My situation is unique. God won't heal me.
In fact, I'm such a bad case that God can't heal me. He can heal every heart but mine.
I'm beyond repair.

In 2 Corinthians 10:4–5 Paul tells us, "The weapons we fight with are not the weapons of the world. On the contrary, they have divine power to demolish strongholds. We demolish arguments and every pretension that sets itself up against the knowledge of God, and we take captive every thought to make it obedient to Christ" (NIV). Instead of having a thought and taking it captive, we often dwell on the thought, nurture it, and water it. Before we know it, a single thought matures into a full-grown belief that we let blossom.

So many of us go through life and never actually *think* about what we're thinking about. I wouldn't have admitted it then, but the day came when I believed my trauma narrative over God's promises. Rather than believing God's truth over my life—the kingdom narrative that proclaims I am his child and nothing can separate me from his love (Rom. 8:35–39)—I accepted the messages from the bad things that had happened to me.

If you had asked me then, never in a million years would I have told you what I heard in my head. I would have told you I believed God's Word over it all. After all, that would be the "right" answer, the "right" thing to say and believe.

But no amount of "right" answers will avert this truth: pain demands to be felt. We can try to bottle it, push it down, avoid it . . . but it will make itself known somewhere, the way water that gets in through a leaky roof can soon start running all over a house, leaving no clue as to where it first started coming in. Unacknowledged pain seeps out into

> *Unacknowledged pain seeps out into our relationships, our habits, our thoughts. It can consume a whole life, like mold growing unseen in the damp darkness of secret spaces.*

our relationships, our habits, our thoughts. It can consume a whole life, like mold growing unseen in the damp darkness of secret spaces.

The toilet is backed up. Again. It has happened often enough now that I know all the usual tricks will do no good.

"I'm going to have to call someone," I tell the three people staying with me for the weekend. They're gracious and understanding, but I'm sure they hadn't bargained on this particular adventure.

Did I mention my sweet little house has only one bathroom? Yes, staying with me is a roll of the dice. This is the third time it's happened while I have visitors. Betting people would find the odds are getting better and better.

Once again I call a plumber for a quick fix. I've had several different guys out, thinking surely one of them will work like magic and vanish the problem forever. I shouldn't be surprised by now, but the total at the bottom of the invoice shocks me every time. An arm, a leg, a lung, and a kidney, all of it.

"If it were my house, I'd be thinking about a whole new system," this one says.

I'm taken back by the cost. I try to buy time instead of new pipes. Even on the day my washing machine backs up, overflows, and spews water across my floors, I still can't bring myself to pay for this and tend to what is screaming for my attention.

My time budget runs out in February 2021. The Great Texas Freeze happens, a weather disaster that cripples the whole state and all of my plumbing. For a while I have no running water at all. And then suddenly I have too much—running in all the wrong places.

My plumber and I crouch near one wall of the house, peering into the dim pier-and-beam crawl space. The home's plumbing is exposed underneath the structure. There is no insulation. He shines a light to point out a few undeniable truths: Many of the pipes have burst. Some of the cast-iron plumbing is 1886 original. And rusty. The newer pipes are, as we would say in Arkansas, "rigged"—propped up on listing cinder blocks, held in place with fraying straps, sagging like snakes on a vine. It's hard to say if the pipes themselves are up to code.

"I doubt it," the plumber says gently, as if to soften the blow.

It is beyond repair.

At some points in my life it was easy to imagine sitting in the ashes with Job after he had lost all of his children, all of his wealth and health and property, all of his servants, and all of his livestock, wondering what had become of his life, his efforts, and his God.

Covered in grime and dust, I could hear Job whisper, "The LORD gave, and the LORD has taken away; blessed be the name of the LORD" (Job 1:21).

This brought me no comfort at all. Was God allowing my suffering too?

Job didn't grieve in the ashes of his life alone. Three of his friends— good friends, close friends, who wept with him and grieved his losses— had plenty to say about the state of his life, why these bad things were happening, and what he should do about it.

Your suffering is your fault.

You need to repent of being evil and try harder to be *good*.

You're lucky it isn't worse.

You should just give up.

You're beyond repair.

God strongly rebuked these men and their thoughts. They had failed to speak the truth about Job, for God himself had said of Job, "There is none like him on the earth, a blameless and upright man, who fears God and turns away from evil" (1:8). Worse, they'd spoken untruths about God. The Lord told them, "You have not spoken of me what is right" (42:7), and demanded their repentance for perpetuating lies. And what is the truth? The Lord himself speaks it to Job and his friends in chapters 38–41: God is unfathomable. And at the bottom of those unfathomable depths, he is love. In the New Testament, the apostle John writes, "God is love. In this the love of God was made manifest among us, that God sent his only Son into the world, so that we might live through him. In this is love, not that we have loved God but that he loved us and sent his Son to be the propitiation for our sins" (1 John 4:8–10).

In the hidden shadows of our lives, any of the lies we believe about God—anything that contradicts the fundamental truth that he is love and he loves us—must be exposed and replaced with the truth. What we believe about God and about ourselves directly affects how we feel. As theologian A. W. Tozer famously wrote, "What comes into our minds when we think about God is the most important thing about us."[1]

> *In the hidden shadows of our lives, any of the lies we believe about God—anything that contradicts the fundamental truth that he is love and he loves us—must be exposed and replaced with the truth.*

Make no mistake, we will always live out what we truly believe. It makes its way down to our bones. I often wonder if this is what David was feeling in Psalm 31:9–10 as he cried out, "Be merciful to me, LORD, for I am in distress; my eyes grow weak with sorrow, my soul and body with grief. My life is consumed by anguish and my years by groaning; my strength fails because of my affliction, and my bones grow weak" (NIV). The King James Version says "my bones are consumed." Have you ever felt a grief, disappointment, sadness that you swore you could feel in your bones? Sometimes we get stuck in cycles of grief instead of passing through them. Our feet get stuck to the floor out of fear, ignorance, powerlessness, or stubbornness. Sometimes all of the above.

The Bible instructs us to take our untrue thoughts and fight them with the truth of God's Word, making each thought obedient to Christ (2 Cor. 10:5). This is a discipline; it doesn't come naturally. I've had times where I've had to do it almost by the hour. Partnering with God in our thoughts is one of the major keys in restoration, the true renewal of our minds. Without this practice and applying these truths, we will continue to live stuck.

I was raised in the South, in westernized American church. Down here, churches are on every corner, and Scriptures are on every marquee and coffee cup. I'm so grateful I was raised with direct access to the Word of God. It's so easy here to get a Bible and read it. But this ease has a

dark side: familiarity. I knew Scriptures by heart and could quote them to you, but in hindsight I question if I really knew them—knew what they meant as living, active words (Heb. 4:12).

The living Word of God has a way of permeating our souls, healing us, restoring us, and making us whole when we let it. Before I really paid attention to the truth of Scripture beyond the easy Christian platitudes, familiarity had created a danger zone in my heart. On hard days I would notice my mind spiraling down . . . down . . . down. Tapes of mental lies would play on a loop in my head, and I had no real biblical tools to stop them. If I paused long enough to *think* about what I was thinking about, I would realize I was rehearsing faulty narratives. But on most days I couldn't do that; I battled deeply with a sense of not being enough, not being truly loved as I was, and not being safe or secure.

On a cold, rainy November morning in 2018, I walked down my driveway to take the trash out. I had gathered all the heavy trash bags and put them in the bins and begun to roll them out to the curb, the thunderous song of the bin wheels loud in my ears as I dragged them. Somehow, a few rough thoughts in my head—old souvenirs that trauma left behind—crept into my body, and I felt like I was having a physical battle. My head was spinning, and it seemed my heart was pounding out of my chest.

Will I ever really get past this pain in my heart and head, or do I have to keep up this juggling act forever?

Will I ever really experience joy and freedom?

I didn't hear an audible voice, but in my spirit I heard a holy whisper. A knowing of something true. It said, "Meshali, which narrative are you going to choose to partner with over your life—trauma's narrative or mine?" At that moment I felt comforted by a sense of unbreakable promise. I had a *choice* in the narrative I believed about my life. I could throw out the untrue thoughts with the trash bins. The tentacles of chemical anxiety and depression aren't ones we can simply discard from our bodies or pretend won't return when we work to cut them off. But through the Spirit's help, I saw that I could choose a better way, the kingdom way. I could embrace the truth, and I could repeat that narrative so often that I believed it more than any other.

I am accepted and loved by God.

I am a child of God (John 1:12).

I am redeemed and forgiven (Col. 1:14).

I am secure in Christ.

I am free from condemnation (Rom. 8:1–2).

I am assured all things will work out (Rom. 8:28).

I cannot be abandoned by God's love (Rom. 8:25–39).

God will finish his good work in me (Phil. 1:6).

I have not been given a spirit of fear (2 Tim. 1:7).

Grace and mercy are always available to me (Heb. 4:16).

This gutting of the lies that lurk in the dark spaces of our lives is not a cruelty but a mercy.

Every heart but mine is loved by God.

Every heart but mine is worthy of love.

Every heart but mine can be healed.

Thoughts like these elevate problems to godlike status. "Every heart but mine" becomes an idol that grows in the soil of our hearts and that we allow to be greater than God. Our hearts are full of needs, especially when they are broken, and we will always seek ways to meet those needs. Idols can only provide false satisfaction: unhealthy relationships when we are lonely, addictions when we are in pain, false identities when we are lost and confused. Only God can meet our deepest needs with the gift of his presence, but first we need to change "but mine" to "and mine":

Every heart and mine *is loved by God.*

Every heart and mine *is worthy of love.*

Every heart and mine *can be healed.*

How do we know this is true?

We know it because God is unfathomable. His ways are higher than ours, and his ways are always for our good.

In February 2020, I visited the Holy Land for the first time. On the fourth evening of our trip, we came to the garden of Gethsemane right before sunset. We had toured all day, and I was tired from walking. As the sun went down, I sat on a small bench that faced the garden straight on, staring into it as our tour guide began teaching us about Jesus's experience there the night before he was crucified.

According to Ray Vander Laan, the word *Gethsemane* is derived from two Hebrew words: *gat*, which means "a place for pressing oil (or wine)," and *shemanim*, which means "oils." The meaning at the root of this important place in Christian history is "press." During Jesus's time, heavy stone slabs were lowered onto olives that had already been crushed in an olive crusher.[2] These fruits, which had been smashed and broken to release their oils, were pressed further.

I can't think of a more accurate description of what Jesus was experiencing.

It's hard to imagine what he felt: the pain, the agony, the fear. He knew what was coming. His life was about to end—violently, with terrible suffering, at the hands of people who hated him and did not understand what he was doing in this world. The Son of God faced arrest, anxiety, grief. His humanity was on full display. Luke the physician records Jesus being in so much agony that "he prayed more earnestly; and his sweat became like great drops of blood falling down to the ground" (Luke 22:44). His prayer was filled with desperation, and he pleaded for some other outcome: "Abba, Father, all things are possible for you. Remove this cup from me. Yet not what I will, but what you will" (Mark 14:36).

In his book *Lent for Everyone*, Bishop N. T. Wright says,

> This scene in Gethsemane is absolutely central to any proper understanding of who Jesus really was. It's all too easy for devout Christians to imagine him as a kind of demigod, striding heroically through the world without a care.

Some have even read John's Gospel that way, though I believe that is to misread it. But certainly Matthew is clear that at this crucial moment Jesus had urgent and agitating business to do with his father. He had come this far; he had told them, again and again, that he would be handed over, tortured and crucified; but now, at the last minute, this knowledge had to make its way down from his scripture-soaked mind into his obedient, praying heart. And it is wonderfully comforting (as the writer to the Hebrews points out) that he had to make this agonizing journey of faith, just as we do.[3]

What is "wonderfully comforting" is that Jesus showed us the way through this valley of the shadow of death: *If there is any other way, Father, please show me what it is!* "Yet," Jesus prayed further, "not what I will, but what you will." Jesus, who was crushed and pressed from all sides, pressed on and pressed through. He knew the suffering that would take place, but he kept his eyes on his Father's sovereignty and his future glory.

We will all come to our Gethsemane. I do believe this. We are crushed in the crossroads—between grief and despair, between faith and hopelessness, between belief that we are children of God or orphans—and we have a choice to make. We can believe what our pain tells us, or we can believe what God says. This is a life-defining moment that requires a crucifying of the flesh, a "not my will but yours be done" moment of truth. We can tell God our little-*t* truth: "Everything in this hurts my flesh, kills my flesh. I need a rescue here!" We can beat on God's chest and announce honestly, "I want to take revenge, not offer forgiveness. I want to get what I need, not give what I have. Don't you see what I'm dealing with here?!"

We can believe what our pain tells us, or we can believe what God says.

And then we can surrender it to him: "I'm choosing what *you* want, Lord, over my own wants and desires. Not my will but yours be done." In Job's case, the prayer sounded like this: "Though he slay me, I will hope in him; yet I will argue my ways to his face" (13:15).

These are hard prayers to pray when we're wounded and bleeding.

I remember a time when the Lord was asking me to forgive someone who had trespassed against me. I was so deeply hurt by their abandonment, the cruel words they'd spoken to me, and the resulting void in my life that I decided it was best for me to mentally write them off. If I could get to a place where they didn't exist in my mind, I reasoned, the pain wouldn't exist either. But God was patient with me while I learned that those hurts don't just leave us, and time doesn't heal all wounds. I had to face them, stop denying them and stuffing them down, stop stewing over the past. I had to see the wrongs for what they were. I had to see the offender's humanness and need for grace. I had to see my own humanness and need for grace. I had to face my pain head-on by forgiving.

Not my will but God's.

Though we all know how hard it can be to trust in the fullness of God's love when we're feeling crushed in Gethsemane, we also know Gethsemane is not the end of the story.

I watch as the plumbing crew restores what was beyond repair with my old pipes. As the hours go by, they shut off the water and drag away all that rigged old junk from under my home. They dig new ditches and haul in brand-new, shiny white pipes that can accommodate freezes. The plumbers place them where they need to be placed, hang them straight, and brace them properly. They add insulation. They turn on the water and . . . it flows properly, smoothly.

Today, everything begins to work as it should. I can feel my stress flow away down that drain. I start doing dishes, washing clothes, and taking showers without incident. I decide to stop thinking twice about inviting guests into my home.

And while it cost me something (a lot of something), it's worth every penny.

"Behold, I am making all things new," John hears God say in his vision of the new heaven and new earth (Rev. 21:5). If God's promise applies to a world crushed by apocalypse, it certainly applies to our individual lives. Will it take work? Yes. Will it cost us something? Yes. But the cost is an investment in our relationship with Christ, and the peace that comes as a result is incalculable.

Now is the moment to stop buying time and living with broken plumbing, as if limping along were the only option available to us. "All things new" is our story with God. In partnering with him through Scripture and Spirit, we will be transformed into the fullness of God's desires for us.

RESTORATION PRACTICE

Take Every Thought Captive to the Truth of Christ

Begin to notice what you are thinking about your life and about God. Second Corinthians 10:5 says, "We demolish arguments and every pretension that sets itself up against the knowledge of God, and we take captive every thought to make it obedient to Christ" (NIV). Begin taking your thoughts captive by writing them down. Be honest. Don't try to hide them or judge them.

Take 2–3 minutes after you wake up and 2–3 minutes before you sleep to write down an answer or two to these questions:

- What does the voice in my head say about God in my life today?
- What statement feels true to me, whether or not it is?

When you take your thoughts captive, start comparing them to Scripture by looking through your Bible or Bible app or doing a quick online search. Beside these captive thoughts, perhaps with a different color pen, write down the truth of what the Bible says. If you're unsure how to search out these truths, ask a minister, counselor, or trusted friend to help you.

3

THE HOUSE
GOD SEES

God Sees You and Looks After You

I'm kneeling in the living room and putting a fresh coat of paint over the old fireplace brick. The freshly painted walls and the wood floors reflect the sunlight and fill the room with hope and expectation.

A century ago, a young couple stood before this fireplace and said their wedding vows. They were Methodist ministers embarking on a new life together, excited to share their own ideas about what home meant to them and how God might bless that vision.

Cindy Carter was this couple's granddaughter and the owner of the home when I bought it. During the process of home buying, Ms. Carter and I never met face-to-face, but we connected with each other via phone and text and quickly discovered our mutual love for Christ.

The property was a sacred special place to Ms. Carter's family, a place they nurtured and were nurtured in. She shared memories with me about her childhood and upbringing here, about the memories her children and grandchildren made. They had sweet times, and some hard times too, within these walls. It was all part of her family's legacy, and she didn't think the story was done being told yet.

"There's still ministry left to be done in that home," she once told me.

I feel honored to grab the baton and be a part of something so rich and beautiful.

As their family evolved and moved to another property, the farmhouse fell into disrepair, but her love for it remained strong. After I took possession of the house and started loving it back to life, I often sent her photos of the work in progress. She followed my journey of restoring each room and blessed the work, sending me texts and Facebook messages telling me she knew God was "pulling off an Ephesians 3:20," something above what we could ask or think. She got so much excitement out of seeing the changes, and her joy blessed me.

I take a break to stretch my back and stand in a square of warm sunlight casting its golden light across the dark wood floor planks. This restoration work always takes longer than we think it will or would like it to. Ms. Carter passed away recently and won't get to see the final results this side of heaven, but I feel her cheering me on. I let the sun wash over my face and close my eyes and think of a story Meredith told me about a dream Ms. Carter shared with her.

In her dream, Ms. Carter came over the hill in front of the house and saw the word *FREEDOM* waving over the roof as if printed on a huge banner hung in the sky and rippling in the wind. She beamed with joy as she told Meredith this story. She told her what she'd later repeat to me: "I do feel in my heart like there is ministry work yet to be fulfilled here."

Not long after my parents announced they were getting a divorce, my mom pulled our car into the driveway of an unfamiliar house in an unfamiliar part of town. It was a tiny little run-down house, and she must have seen the hesitation in my eyes as she parked. Everything about my life had become strange and confusing.

"Meshali, I promise we are going to fix it up," she said. "We can work on it and make it our own. Give me a few months, and it will look so much better."

What could I say? I was twelve. My whole world had been turned on its side. The old familiar feelings of safety and comfort seemed to be gone. To my adolescent mind and heart, this house embodied all those scary feelings.

To this day, the thought of that house is a bag of mixed feelings and memories in my hindsight. Many of them are good, but a lot are sad and hard. Life's blows hit us all—all of my family members—shattering our hearts in ways that felt irreparable. Our lot faced many troubles, including money problems, addiction issues, and mental health battles, that had never been part of my life before we moved there.

As we sat in the driveway of this strange house that I couldn't call home, God saw my longing before I knew how to name it myself, when I could only sense an "ache for something I cannot name," as American psychologist Lauren Slater so poignantly put it.[1] When I knew that I wanted something like stability and safety and security, God knew I was actually feeling homesick, because even at that early age I felt that home was something the enemy of my soul took from me.

Trauma had brought me so much shame that secrecy became my survival. I locked that shame-filled room of my heart up tight and threw away the key, believing I could—no, I *had to*—go on with my life without allowing God into that room. What would he see there? Disarray, disrepair, despair.

I tried to hide the shame. When it came to hiding it from people, I was often successful. But God can't be fooled. He sees those locked rooms and knows what's behind the doors. But even our all-knowing and powerful God will not force his way into a room. He waits for us. He doesn't broadcast our dirty laundry and make a public spectacle of overnight transformations.

God's restoration work is a process that is partly dependent on our willingness to stay open to his timing.

In the charismatic faith tradition I was raised in and dearly love, a whole lot of value was placed on the "big moments" of a Christian experience: the powerful testimonies, the miraculous healings, the thunder-and-lightning encounters with the Spirit. I'll be the first to say the events of our faith life matter, starting with the decision to invite God to become Lord of our lives. But I also know God's restoration work is a process that is partly dependent on our willingness to stay open to his timing, to not close ourselves off to him. That moment when we open the secret doors to God, nervously asking him to come in and help us clean up, is only the first of many, many experiences that might not be accompanied by much fanfare.

So he waited for me to open up the door and invite him in to do the dirty work of cleaning, repairing, restoring. Since I had cracked the door open that day in Peggy's office, she had been helping me push it wider, inviting God and others in by degrees. With her guidance, I did the work I could do and entrusted the rest to God.

On a beautiful December day in 2017, before the run-down farm-house became mine, I packed up my overnight bag and photo gear and loaded my Jeep, headed for a job in Austin's beautiful Hill Country. It was the perfect day for a shoot, and the piercing blue Texas sky was my backdrop. I was riding down I-35, taking in the vivid greens and blues outside my windows. I remember the feeling I had as I drove, the contradiction of the outdoor beauty versus the pain that seemed to come and go in my gut.

Everything in my life that day looked fine from the outside. I was thriving. My career as a photographer was evolving and taking off. I was taking on fewer weddings and doing more portrait photography—an art I especially loved. I was getting an increasing amount of work shooting influential people—artists, authors, and musicians, especially in Christian circles. The Lord brought incredible people into my path, some who have become my dearest of friends. I began seeing my work on cover after cover in bookstores, swelling my insides with joy and my eyes with tears as I walked past.

Even as a recovering perfectionist, the instinct to always appear okay was alive and well. I constantly felt the need to be "on." Some days okay wasn't even enough—I had to appear *better* than okay, like I was on top of the world. Oddly, the more I accomplished, the more I became aware of a gaping hole in me, and it was getting wider by the year. Somewhere deep inside, beyond my ability to track down myself, was a hole I could never seem to fill.

Peggy and I had talked about this. I was actively processing it, praying about it, and trying to get to the bottom of it all. She reminded me there would be tougher seasons even in healing, and to walk through them with Jesus, not to shy away from him and his love for me. I began to realize and accept it was those very places of weakness, wounds, and

inabilities where God wanted to show me his strength. In 2 Corinthians 12:9 Paul tells us, "He said to me, 'My grace is sufficient for you, for my power is made perfect in weakness.' Therefore I will boast all the more gladly about my weaknesses, so that Christ's power may rest on me" (NIV). I was coming into a new realization about myself and about the Christian journey: Christ is drawn toward our neediness, not our great performance. He is drawn into our need for him, the places in life that feel like impossibilities. Again and again, we invite him into these places and his power shows up. Sometimes quietly and over many, many years.

That December day as I drove in the Hill Country, the old familiar sadness I couldn't seem to shake crept up on me like a homesick yearning.

Christ is drawn toward our neediness, not our great performance.

My heart needed roots. I had just entered my thirties and was tired of renting. At the time, my "home" was a little loft tucked right in the heart of the city, Mockingbird Station in Dallas. I had wanted to live in the city at least once in my life to experience the so-called magic I'd heard of. The loft sat about six floors directly above a Starbucks, which I frequented every morning on my way out to work. Right across the street was my favorite furniture store, West Elm. Every day felt like an adventure. I quickly found out the city life wasn't for me. The hustle and bustle, the nonstop traffic, the blaring horns and bright lights were a bit much for a highly sensitive person like myself. My Arkansas upbringing shone through, and my heart longed for open spaces, a front porch, and a true haven of comfort where it could be still and quiet. I wanted a home of my own, a place to settle down in, dig deep, and plant myself. I craved it.

Once, right before my lease came to an end, I remember standing in my apartment while facing out the huge open wall of windows that overlooked the city. I felt so small in this huge city of people, everyone living their lives with their lattes and briefcases. Everyone seems so sure of their lives and what they're doing when you know nothing about them. And they sure did as I watched them walking by that day. I certainly didn't feel that way. I stood there wondering, "Where to next for me, God?"

That old nagging question crept up in my mind again: "Do you see me here, God?"

Pastor Rhonda Davis is someone who has been a great encourager in my life. She has always reminded me that "God has a million ways to work, and all we have is one, and that is to trust him." One morning she texted me and said, "Meshali, I really sense the Lord is going to give you roots and wings." Her statement brought my focus back to the main thing I was in need of—real trust in God. He often is working behind the scenes in ways we can't see. I thought, "Roots and wings? How so? Lord, what does that even mean?" In the middle of my questioning, I moved forward and just did the next right thing. I continued on in my shoots as I was making some big decisions about where to next.

As I set out to the Hill Country, my maps led me to take a right onto a little gravel road that took me back to a quaint Airbnb tucked away behind the hills and trees. The sun had set, and I had a big day ahead of me, so I decided to go to bed a little earlier than usual. As I slept that night, I had a dream that changed the trajectory of my life.

Now, I feel the need to preface this dream by saying I am not a person who dreams all the time, nor do I call every dream a "prophetic dream." I hold that phrase, which is sometimes carelessly thrown around, with both great reverence and healthy skepticism. I was raised Pentecostal—I know how bizarre some prophetic dreams can seem, trust me. Several people have told me of dreams *they've* had about my life and future, and if I took time to share the weird, kooky ones here, I don't know if we would all laugh or cry. However, I do strongly believe that God can speak to us in visions and dreams and powerfully use them to bring us direction, hope, and encouragement.

In my dream, I stood facing the run-down home where I had spent some of the harder years of my childhood. In the blink of an eye, the house came down, and I saw a beautiful home being built on the lot. This new home came up from the ground with indescribable light in and around it; the colors that touched everything were so vivid and bright—even the grass and trees.

The Holy Spirit sometimes speaks to us in the love languages of our hearts, and so many symbols of mine appeared before my dreaming eyes. The white house had a porch across the front, wooden beams, and lots of windows to let the light in. As I watched the house coming up slowly, I took notice of three men busy at work. One man was on the roof, one man was working on the windows, and one man knelt at the base of one of the wooden beams on the front porch and was nailing a board down on the deck. He looked up at me, waved kindly, and smiled.

I woke from the dream suddenly, startled to discover myself still there in that little Hill Country cabin. I knew immediately that the dream was symbolic of something God was wanting to do in my life and heart. I felt a true *knowing*, a sense that God was speaking to me about so much more than a physical house.

In *Mere Christianity*, C. S. Lewis urged readers:

Imagine yourself as a living house. God comes in to rebuild that house. At first, perhaps, you can understand what He is doing. He is getting the drains right and stopping the leaks in the roof and so on; you knew that those jobs needed doing and so you are not surprised. But presently He starts knocking the house about in a way that hurts abominably and does not seem to make any sense. What on earth is He up to? The explanation is that He is building quite a different house from the one you thought of—throwing out a new wing here, putting on an extra floor there, running up towers, making courtyards. You thought you were being made into a decent little cottage: but He is building a palace. He intends to come and live in it Himself.[2]

Even then I understood God was reminding me that he is making all things new, restoring me as a living house. He was doing a deep work in me, refashioning the rooms of my heart. He was moving, restoring, and bringing life back to spaces I had closed off, dusting down the cobwebs, pulling back the curtains, and throwing open the windows to let in air and light.

As I've gotten older, I've been able to see a more aerial view of my childhood and the people in it. I've been granted the grace and perspective to see everyone's place and part on the stage of life. In other words, I'm being set free.

Proverbs 13:12 says, "Hope deferred makes the heart sick, but a longing fulfilled is a tree of life" (NIV). God saw my longing. God saw me traveling around the world, working, coming and going, and knew I needed an anchor point, a North Star, a place to come back to over and over again. A place where I can find my belongings, my projects, my work, my people. A place that is always waiting for me.

Maybe the depth of our need and suffering correlate to the degree of gratitude and joy we feel when God meets our truest longings. I had no idea how owning my little fixer-upper home—how having a place of my own to plant, settle, and build—would bring healing to my heart. As I do the work on the building, God does the work on my soul.

But he saw more than my longing. He saw *me*. Jesus knows not just our wants, but he knows and desires to give us what we truly need, even if it's different from what we expect. When Hagar was cast out of her home by Sarai, I wonder if she thought she would die pregnant and alone in the desert. But God saw Hagar and instructed her to return to Sarai—probably the last thing she thought she wanted. But Hagar's relief is evident in her response: "So she called the name of the LORD who spoke to her, 'You are a God of seeing,' for she said, 'Truly here I have seen him who looks after me'" (Gen. 16:13).

I am being looked after, and so are you, by the Father, his Son, and his Spirit—the architect, the carpenter, and the designer of our lives. It's time for us to open the door of our heart-home a little wider to each of them.

> *Jesus knows not just our wants, but he knows and desires to give us what we truly need, even if it's different from what we expect.*

RESTORATION PRACTICE

Come Out of Hiding and Invite God to See You

Do you dare allow God to see you? When God looks at you, he doesn't see your failures, your sins, your mistakes, or your shortcomings. He sees you in the Beloved—he sees you in Christ, and he sees the blood that has been shed for you. Because of this, his thoughts toward you are thoughts of loving-kindness, forgiveness, blessing, and favor.

Grab a pen and a notebook and draw a vertical line down the center of one page, writing at the top of the left column "What I See" and at the top of the right column "What God Sees." First, take a few minutes to write your honest feelings about yourself—*who you are*, the good or the hard—in the "What I See" column. Then take a moment and write out a correlating "What God Sees" message on the other side. Utilize Scripture and prayer and even past conversations with trusted mentors as you consider what God sees.

Turning your face to God so he can gaze upon you, with all your longings and all your feelings of shame or despair, requires no special prayer, no special formula, no trumpets or spotlights. All that's required is a willing heart and the belief that God will do as much as you allow him to.

PART 2

REPAIR

4

WHAT RESTORATION MEANS

You Are Being Re-storied and Made New

The kitchen is an absolute mess. Tons of old sheetrock and pieces of the farmhouse's history are spread all over the floor. I kneel down, peeling back some of the linoleum. The air is filled with dust and I'm pouring sweat. May in Texas is already heating up, and everyone I know is feeling it. These layers of life peeling off the walls are anything but pretty, and on this big demo day everything is in a state of upheaval and disrepair. These circumstances aren't exactly ideal for my personality type.

My contractor yells my name from the home's only bathroom. He's been working in there for hours.

"Meshali, can you come take a look in here?"

My house is so small he starts talking to me before I get to him. "What do you want to do in here, you think? What do you see for this space?"

From the hallway I can see the single-hung window with its frosted glass, allowing beautiful morning light in. The sink and toilet are gone. The beautiful clawfoot tub is out temporarily. It will go back in after being refreshed. He has ripped up the flooring and removed the old rough wood paneling from the walls. It takes only a fraction of a second for me to take all this in before my eyes lock on the last thing I had ever expected to see.

I stand out in the hall in absolute disbelief, unable to answer his question or hear anything else he is saying.

That ugly, splintering paneling had been hiding wallpaper. I stare at maroon roses, pink primroses, and hunter-green leafy vines on a

background that might have been white once upon a time. It's too stained to be sure, covered in mildew and grime.

This is the first time I have seen this wallpaper in this house. But I have definitely seen that print before.

In a flash, a flood of memories rises up and carries me away on a rushing current back to a place I do not want to be: the bathroom decorated with identical paper in my childhood home, the one that I had dreamed about. A huge mix of emotions washes over me.

The contractor is talking but I don't hear his words. The static of shock has drowned out all other noise. Oddly, I sense that God is right next to me. For this bizarre slice of time he and I stand in the bathrooms—both of them at the same time, here in the present and there in the past—alone.

I gave these hard memories over to you, I say to him.

You did. I have them.

Then why . . . ? These are the only two words I have.

How can he allow this? I thought I'd been freed of these memories that marked me. Will I be handcuffed to them forever? Did I not pray the right words before?

Sometimes when I think about restoration I think about the man with the withered hand. "Stretch out your hand," Jesus said to him. And we're told, "He stretched it out, and his hand was restored" (Mark 3:5). Just like that. One second his hand was deformed, and the next it was completely new.

Much like with a home, my experience of soul restoration has taken—and continues to take—much longer than I'd like. Over the years I've become more comfortable with this. When things I'm dealing with don't just miraculously vanish from my life, I've learned to ask the Lord an earnest question: *God, what are you teaching me through this?*

I've learned all kinds of things through that one question. I've learned to trust God more and to rely on him for strength and wisdom. I've learned that only he can save me, that no earthly answers exist to certain problems, and that he is my friend that sticks closer than a brother when others walk away.

We often pray for the mending or healing of something broken in our lives, something we can usually see, touch, or feel. Our broken hearts, broken relationships, broken families, broken bodies. We want healing, restoration, relief—we want this *more* than we want wisdom, and we want it fast. If we trust in God as our all-knowing Father, he will produce fruits in us that are a reflection of his strength and godliness (2 Pet. 1:3). Our strengths, weaknesses, and trials all work together for our good when placed in his hands.

We sometimes try to pray away things in our lives that have to be lived and walked out in order to bear fruit.

We sometimes try to pray away things in our lives that have to be lived and walked out in order to bear fruit. James instructs us to be joyful even in times of intense trial: "Count it all joy, my brothers, when you meet trials of various kinds, for you know that the testing of your faith produces steadfastness. And let steadfastness have its full effect, that you may be perfect and complete, lacking in nothing. If any of you lacks wisdom, let him ask God, who gives generously to all without reproach, and it will be given him" (1:2–5).

There's no getting around it. The path to becoming "perfect and complete, lacking in nothing" runs straight through hard times.

But the good news is that we don't travel alone. When I stood in that bathroom and faced that wallpaper, God made it plain to me that he was near, that this was not a mistake. I call these moments "God winks." They don't always happen, and we don't get to always live life with such crystal clarity, but in that moment he spoke to me so clearly and gave me the gift of a reminder.

"Meshali," he said, "I was with you then. I'm with you now. I'm making all things new."

I've heard it said that in the kingdom of God, to be restored is to receive back more than what has been lost. The ultimate state is greater than the original condition, and something or someone has been improved beyond measure. Job got back twice what he had lost. Joseph was promoted from slave to Pharaoh's right-hand man. Jesus healed bodies so they could do what they had never done before. In earthly terms, restoration brings something back to its original intent—like the deformed hand that Jesus healed. But I believe anything we put in Jesus's care becomes not just new but better than new.

God's original intent for humankind was unity with him. God placed Adam and Eve in the garden of Eden in absolute bliss and paradise. He set them in a beautiful, perfect place full of promise and safety. He gave them just one boundary, which they chose to cross. And when they did, they broke that perfect unity with God. Sin and death, disorder and darkness, and shame entered the world. Jesus paid the price to redeem us and reverse the separation. He made a way for us to be restored to unity with God, not just while we walk the earth but in eternity too.

God always has a redemption plan. From Genesis to Revelation, God's heart for restoration rings true. While this is a story for all of humanity, it very much mirrors my particular story of a child whose home life was happy and whole, then broken by sin and loss. As a twelve-year-old girl, I experienced the devastation at a crucial time of physical, emotional, and spiritual development. During that time of my life, I was merely surviving.

I knew the saving grace of Jesus, but I still had to walk through tough stuff. Church was a safe place for me. I attended the First Assembly of God in El Dorado, Arkansas, and it became a place that deeply shaped me and my identity for the better. Despite that, I still struggled to know who I really was. Though I knew Jesus was with me, my heart felt shattered. All the heavy weights and anxieties I carried multiplied within me, but I couldn't find comfort in God (Ps. 94:19).

For a while I resented the story God handed me. I resented the story of the way my life had unfolded, the people in it, the poor ways I responded to my circumstances. I slipped into regret and bitterness, and these emotions ate away at me. I felt I'd been set up at a disadvantage, and that led me to feel dead on the inside. Instead of taking those feelings to Jesus, I tried to stuff them down.

I didn't realize I did this. It was just how I coped, how I survived. I didn't know that if I partnered with God's kingdom narrative, even the hardships could serve me well. What is the kingdom narrative? It is the story of our hardships and wounds being healed for God's glory and the betterment of the world. The story of my life, the whole story—the good, the hard, the in-between—could be rewritten.

God offers us not only the gift of being restored but also the gift of being *re-storied*. God invites us into partnership with him. In him, we embrace the new story he has written—one of living restored ourselves and of then being able to give others a road map through their own pain. This map of hope says we can and will overcome trauma. We will see brighter days and live a life of joy and peace, of promise and deep fulfillment.

In Christ, we are no longer defined by the terrible things that have been done to us. In Christ, we are no longer victims but victors. In Christ, our hardships and struggles can be transformed into wisdom, empathy, courage, and compassion for others. Our lives can tell the tale of glory. All we have to do is accept God's invitation to step into a restored identity—a *restoration* identity.

Who do you think you are?

As we each attempt to answer that for ourselves, we often default to how we see ourselves. But just like we saw in the previous chapter's restoration practice of comparing what I see with what God sees, it's crucial to answer that through the lens of how *God* sees us. It is the one who created us who gets to identify us and name us. We are marked by and made in the image of God, the imago Dei (Gen. 1:27).

> For you formed my inward parts;
>   you knitted me together in my mother's womb.
> I praise you, for I am fearfully and wonderfully made.
> Wonderful are your works;
>   my soul knows it very well.

My frame was not hidden from you,
when I was being made in secret,
    intricately woven in the depths of the earth.
Your eyes saw my unformed substance;
in your book were written, every one of them,
    the days that were formed for me,
        when as yet there was none of them. (Ps. 139:13–16)

We live in a world of filtered, fictional images. As a photographer, I can recognize how images are altered, how their integrity has been compromised. The filter that I choose to place on a photo can shift the whole image. I can change the color, the exposure, the details. I can distort an image and create effects that were never there in reality. The wrong filter can distort an image into something it never was, and AI advancements are taking image filtering and image creation to whole new levels. Filters ultimately make us feel bad. Think about that for a second—something that isn't real has the power to make us feel bad about ourselves! Here's the truth: What God made doesn't need to be changed.

Sometimes other photographers who have seen and admired my work ask me to teach them my editing process. The overwhelming majority of them use a popular postediting filter system that they apply almost universally to their images. They're surprised when I tell them I have a very different method: I don't use any software but edit every image by hand so I can preserve its true beauty. I treat every image as unique. Yes, it's a time-consuming process, but it honors my subjects and is part of my brand.

For me this isn't a marketing gimmick. I want to capture the world as it really is. If it's not the real thing, it's not the true story. If it's not the true story, it doesn't bear the image of God. The only filter we need to see ourselves through is the filter of God's truth.

Our understanding of our identity starts and ends with our understanding of who God is and who he says we are. Period. That period seems abrupt. At times everything in me wants to add a *but*. Except there is no *but*. The truth is sealed: I am a child of God. "But now thus says the

Lord, he who created you, O Jacob, he who formed you, O Israel: 'Fear not, for I have redeemed you; I have called you by name, you are mine'" (Isa. 43:1). This is not only a promise for the Israelites. The apostle John wrote, "See what kind of love the Father has given to us, that we should be called children of God; and so we are" (1 John 3:1).

The only filter we need to see ourselves through is the filter of God's truth.

I am chosen, loved, accepted, valued, championed by my Father. And so are you. I have frequently had to whisper that (and sometimes yell it) to myself: "I am a child of God!" When we begin to live *from* our true identity—who Christ has said we are—and not *for* some identity defined by the world's filters, we are empowered to walk in the fullness of all God has for us.

Our identity is secure when we receive Christ and walk in Christ. Receive the identity he has spoken over you by holding the exercise from chapter 3 close and examining exactly what God sees. Believe it. We don't work to earn this seat at his family table; it's there, waiting for us to take it and live from it.

The following passage from Ephesians 2 has transformed me. Pay attention to the posture Paul mentions.

> But God, being rich in mercy, because of the great love with which he loved us, even when we were dead in our trespasses, made us alive together with Christ—by grace you have been saved—and raised us up with him and *seated us with him* in the heavenly places in Christ Jesus, so that in the coming ages he might show the immeasurable riches of his grace in kindness toward us in Christ Jesus. For by grace you have been saved through faith. And this is not your own doing; it is the gift of God, not a result of works, so that no one may boast. For we are his workmanship, created in Christ Jesus for good works, which God prepared beforehand, that we should walk in them. (vv. 4–10)

We are seated with Christ. That sounds like a place of assurance to me, a place of unshakable identity. Not one of striving or lack but of rest and security. These verses also speak of the great love of the Father. When we were dead in sin—not when we were shiny and worthy—*he* made us alive and raised us up, and now we *are* seated with him. Right now.

We are daughters and sons of God living in a broken world. We often hear that we are to be in this world but not of it, yet unfortunately the pains and woundings of this life still hit us. As soon as we take our first breath, we are subject to the brokenness of the world. Despite our best efforts, we can't protect ourselves or even the ones we dearly love from it. The promise of a true identity is our sure anchor in the midst of heartache and brokenness. This identity is a gift from God. A whole new identity, a new name.

Even on days I don't feel like a daughter of God, I am.

Being a child of God is not something that can be earned or achieved. As a person who has tended to strive and earn, this thought has been one that I've had to come to know, believe, and accept through the help of the Holy Spirit. Even on days I don't feel like a daughter of God, I am. Not because of anything I do, have done, or will do, but because of Christ. Only Christ.

On my shelf of "special things" in my home, I keep a kintsugi vase. The Japanese art of kintsugi has always spoken deeply to me. I first heard of it when I was at the Nashville Rescue Mission in 2019 listening to its president, Rev. Glenn Cranfield, talk about a few of his ministry encounters with people experiencing homelessness. Rev. Glenn's talk made my heart feel like it was on fire. I sensed the love of God all over him as he talked about his experiences; I saw Jesus in him.

He talked about one of the precious girls he ministered to and how he began to ask her to come to the mission. He told her Jesus loved her and that if she came, she would be cared for—clothed and fed and given a place of shelter. She resisted the offer time and time again.

One day as she passed by, she asked Rev. Glenn in a sarcastic but curious tone, "So you mean to tell me that if I come to this shelter, this Jesus will make me better?"

Rev. Glenn lovingly said, "Jesus won't make you better, he will make you new. Better than new." She agreed to come, and her life was changed in that place.

My heart was touched as he shared this story and other powerful testimonies. He held up a cup that had been broken and reassembled. The repair lines were visible. No attempt at all had been made to hide the breaks. He said, "This is kind of like you and me, huh? None of us are any different." He explained how the art of kintsugi uses gold to mend broken vessels. The restored product is stronger and more beautiful than ever before.

My soul burned as he talked. *That's it. That's what I feel like God is doing in my life.* I immediately purchased my own piece of kintsugi art as a visual reminder that Christ mends the brokenhearted.

I stand inside my gutted bathroom, still staring at the wall. It's 2018, but in some ways I'm still the same little girl who stood looking at the same wallpaper in another bathroom thirty years ago. Except now I have a hammer and paintbrush in my hand.

We strip as much of it away as possible, but shreds of it stubbornly remain. After all, the experiences of life don't vanish at will. I watch as he pulls back the final piece. A bit of dust floats through the air of that tiny bathroom. Bits of old rotting wood crumble to the ground.

Later, I pore over a book of what seems like a million paint swatches. I point to a beautiful creamy white.

"That's the one for the bathroom," I say. "I love that shade."

I look at the name: *Alabaster.*

Before I know it, fresh sheetrock covers the remaining shreds of paper. On the day we paint it, the sun is shining and golden light cascades through the bathroom window. We put up big, wide strokes of the beautiful white paint, and with each pass of the roller I begin to see it: The room is being made new. Clean. A blank slate to build upon. It means more to me than anyone there really knows—this symbol of God's redemption for me, his story crashing into mine.

God is always with us, closer than our very breath, but sometimes he gives us tangible reminders of just how close and present he is. Such God winks are like visual, physical representations of what Christ is saying to us or doing in us.

My dream is becoming reality in this house. Restoration isn't just about the tearing down; mostly, it's about the building up.

What comes back up when God's in it is always better than new.

RESTORATION PRACTICE

Set Aside Your Old Identity to Embrace Your Restoration Identity

Before painting my bathroom in Alabaster White, I wrote 1 Peter 5:10–11 on one of the pieces of wallpaper that stayed glued to the wall: "In his kindness God called you to share in his eternal glory by means of Christ Jesus. So after you have suffered a little while, he will restore, support, and strengthen you, and he will place you on a firm foundation. All power to him forever! Amen" (NLT). Any worldly identity we establish for ourselves, whether it comes from pride or from shame, doesn't share Christ's eternal glory. We only get that in him.

Identify something that represents your old identity—maybe a photograph, a certificate or award, or any token of your particular pain and heartbreak—and write on it one of the Scripture references from this chapter that reminds you of your true identity in Christ. Above all, you *are* a child of God.

5

THE MASTER
CARPENTER

You Never Have to Fix or Face Anything Alone

The darkest room of my house is the one at its heart. Due to the quirkiness of the way this old home was built, you have to walk through this passageway room to get from one end of the house to the other. There's no way around it. I dread letting people see it, but short of taking them outside and around it, they have to come through here. It's definitely not the room I'll be showcasing on Instagram anytime soon.

I suppose it's a hallway of sorts. In fact it's a former run-off porch that was enclosed at some point. The chocolate-colored hardwood floors are completely buckled in the middle because the foundation has shifted so much over time. Visitors jokingly call this the speed bump. Not even counting that warp, the whole floor slants toward the back of the house. The roof is weathered tin that also slants down to the edge of the roofline. Gosh, it's in bad shape. The worst shape of any area in this home that I've owned for only a few weeks.

I stand in the center of this cavern and turn in a slow circle. I smell dust, mildew, and rotting wood. All four walls are boarded up, covering the windows, but some boards are missing. I see old wallpaper behind the gaps. This room is going to have to be completely rebuilt.

Meshali, what have you gotten yourself into?

The work feels too big, too expensive, too much of a headache, impossible in ways. How will I ever fully restore a whole home if just one room overwhelms me?

I fill my lungs with a slow, deep breath. There's only one way I know of: I will redo this room by room, piece by piece, step-by-step. And I can do it myself.

For most of my life I have been a master fixer. I don't really know why. It might be partly related to my personality, partly to my role as firstborn child, partly to my learned life experiences. Whatever the reason, when things go sideways, my first instinct is to fix them, clean them, and make all well and peaceful again. Sitting in a mess is so uncomfortable I can hardly stand it.

I didn't do this only for myself but for everyone around me too.

Hurting from a broken relationship? I'll offer every hopeful word and ounce of empathy I've got.

Dealing with a medical problem? I'll help you research treatments.

Confronting a crisis of faith? I'll encourage you daily until you reach the other side.

You get the picture.

Unfortunately, too often these efforts are merely cosmetic. They make the cracks pretty but never expose the foundational problem. There were areas of my life I thought were good and "fixed"—until the tiniest shift would throw me off-center. A harsh word from a friend, a lack of affirmation from someone I trusted, a relationship complication, a disappointment . . . you name it, it would trigger me.

Whenever I felt scared or not in control of a situation, I would jump into action without stopping to ask myself what I was scared of. I'd just start trying to create order in my life. I would clean the house, set up a new schedule or new habits, try on new systems to manage my workload and projects. I looked for new ways to make sure everyone I knew was okay, happy, cared for. I worked and worked, pouring a lot of energy into getting disorder and discomfort out of my life. These efforts went a long way toward easing the anxiety and chaos in my soul.

But only for a little while. In time, there I was again—exhausted and frustrated.

I'm sure I'm not the only one who tries to fix deep problems with behaviors that can only polish the surface of our lives. We try to solve serious internal issues with external behaviors. We try to treat the fruit for diseases that start at the root.

Every fruit has a root. In my case, all of my fix-it efforts were rooted in a belief that I was unworthy of love and care. I felt if I could just be good enough—and not just good enough but the BEST—at fixing my life and helping others do the same, I could earn self-worth and value like a sticker on a chart.

When we stop to ask ourselves "What's at the root of this issue?" then we find our true needs and desires. Needs are not wrong. We are human beings, and pain demands to be felt. Even if we don't consciously acknowledge these needs, our minds and bodies will try to satisfy them. So spending time examining them is important. The Lord longs to meet us in these secret spaces. We can't hide them from him.

"I wish you'd let me fix that for you," he is saying. "I wish you'd let me meet that need."

The fact that there were three men in my long-ago dream has never been lost on me. As I've come to think of myself as a "living house," I've pondered that vivid dream of the men restoring a home. To me, their identities are clear.

The man on the roof symbolized strength and protection, a covering. He is God the Father—my protector, my shield, my safety. He is our ever-present help in times of trouble (Ps. 46:1). He is the architect of my life, the one who knows everything about me and what I'm going through. He is the shelter to come under when life's harsh weather hits, for "he who dwells in the shelter of the Most High will abide in the shadow of the Almighty. I will say to the LORD, 'My refuge and my fortress, my God, in whom I trust'" (Ps. 91:1–2).

The man at the windows that filled the house with warm, comforting light represented the Holy Spirit. Jesus promised his disciples, "The Father . . . will give you another advocate to help you and be with you forever—the Spirit of truth. The world cannot accept him, because it neither sees him nor knows him. But you know him, for he lives with you and will be in you" (John 14:16–17 NIV). God's Spirit in me shines the light of truth into the dark spaces of my life and fills them not with

accusation or condemnation but freedom, life, and hope. He is the designer, showing off the full potential of my life's beauty when I don't try to hide in darkness.

And the man on the porch who smiled at me was Jesus, who took the identity of a carpenter while on this earth. He walked this physical life of heartache and joy and knows all its ups and downs. He knows exactly what I'm going through. "Since then we have a great high priest who has passed through the heavens, Jesus, the Son of God, let us hold fast our confession," said the writer of Hebrews. "For we do not have a high priest who is unable to sympathize with our weaknesses, but one who in every respect has been tempted as we are, yet without sin. Let us then with confidence draw near to the throne of grace, that we may receive mercy and find grace to help in time of need" (Heb. 4:14–16). I have always loved this Scripture because it reminds me not only of God's power but that he was touched with "the feeling of our infirmities" (KJV). Jesus, whose name Immanuel means "God with us," lowered himself to see eye to eye with you and me. Jesus the carpenter is not just a sympathizer but also a stabilizer, the great leveler and empathizer. When I think of that great wooden beam he was securing at the porch, I recognize this as faithful work he is doing in the foundations of my life.

Room by room, piece by piece, the Father, Son, and Holy Spirit are working on our behalf and healing us.

Together the Father, Son, and Holy Spirit are restoring broken places. Room by room, piece by piece, the Father, Son, and Holy Spirit are working on our behalf and healing us. Not only to our original state, but to better than new. I promise they're doing the same for you. Because the truth is, if God is not the one building the house, our efforts will always be in vain (Ps. 127:1).

~

Late one night I lay awake in bed thinking about the pain that a family member of mine was facing. My family has been touched in several ways by the hellish grip of addiction. This particular family member was facing crisis, and my heart ached. As bad as I wanted to, I couldn't fix this. I was powerless to fix it. Through the night, I tossed and turned and asked the Lord to help them.

Jesus, be near to them. Jesus, work in their life and heart in ways that only you can.

The more I tossed and turned and cycling thoughts stirred in my brain, the more tired I got. But I couldn't sleep. I said to the Lord, "Please help me, Lord. I am worried and carrying this burden in a way that I know you don't want me to. I trust you. I trust your power. I believe, but help my unbelief. Please help me with the part of my own heart that has trouble trusting, the part that is triggered by the pain of addiction in those I love because of how deeply it has affected me. Heal me, Lord, in areas where I myself need it . . ."

My heart felt overwhelmed. But I felt Jesus speak to my heart and say, "I understand. I know the pain of being overwhelmed. I have felt it too." I felt the love of the Lord wash over me. As I thought of how Christ became flesh and dwelt among us, how he was touched with the feelings of humanity, I found comfort. He had also been overwhelmed and in pain. He understood. And he had overcome all of that.

Jesus knows and he cares. He prays for me (John 17:9). There's no one I'd rather have praying for me than Jesus. As I lay there that night and these thoughts washed over me, they brought me great comfort, as they always do whenever I face a pain that is unbearable or a responsibility that is too much to handle. I chose to rest in the anchoring truth that I myself don't have to fix it or do it, but he has promised to carry me and be my help.

And I finally fell asleep.

Before I could feel *known*, I needed to know Jesus.

Jesus made himself known to me in a real way at a young age, and I had a hunger to want to know more of him. I was the kid who was at church every time the doors would open. We had Sunday morning and evening services, Tuesday night prayer, and Wednesday night church.

Every time the people met, my heart wanted to be there. The family of God is a beautiful community, and these folks were my second family.

On a Sunday morning in 1995, when I was twelve, I made a personal decision to follow Jesus. I remember that Sunday morning so vividly I can still smell the cedar pews. My church had four sections of wooden pews, and I was in the third row from the front on a left side section. I'd sat through many sermons, but there was something different about the one Brother Ronnie preached that morning. I honestly don't even remember what the sermon was about. But I remember the feeling I had, the way the Holy Spirit tugged at my heartstrings and drew me in.

The Lord's tangible love swept over me like a tidal wave. When Brother Ronnie gave the invitation to come forward and accept Jesus, I couldn't stay put. I shot up out of my seat and walked forward with a tender heart to receive Jesus for myself. Even at twelve and having been raised in a ministry family, I needed to own my relationship with him. I knew I needed a Savior. I was drawn to commit my life to him based not on anyone else's walk with the Lord but my own.

Through my teen years, the Lord continued to draw me in tenderly, going behind and before me in the trauma and post-trauma seasons I lived through. I purchased a teen study Bible with a shiny tie-dyed print on the cover, and for the first time I began to read through the New Testament and understand it. I read at night by my little nightlight, snug in the space between my bed and the wall. I started in the book of Matthew and just kept reading. Jesus was building something in me at that time that would sustain me in those years specifically and in the years to come. The seeds that were being planted in me through the reading of Scripture and the love of my church community and youth group would be nurtured and blossom into a safe place I could run to again and again. I'm so grateful for this grace early on in my life, not because it made my life easy but because it helped me to find my footing in later years when it became clear that the Lord was my only path to restoration.

I've always loved the story found in John 11 of Jesus raising Lazarus from the dead. It's a familiar story told often in Sunday school. I can relate to the crying out of Mary and Martha, who had such clear grief over the death of their brother. "Lord, if you had been here, my brother would not have died," Martha accused Jesus when he finally showed up days after they called for him (v. 21). Mary and Martha didn't question Jesus's power or ability to heal. They questioned where he was.

When I was suffering, where were you, Jesus?

How could you allow this trauma to happen to me, God?

Mary and Martha's situation must have felt beyond hopeless, but they took their grief and questions to the feet of Jesus, and he met them with compassion and power.

Verses 33–35 have always spoken to me: "When Jesus saw her weeping, and the Jews who had come with her also weeping, he was deeply moved in his spirit and greatly troubled. And he said, 'Where have you laid him?' They said to him, 'Lord, come and see.' Jesus wept."

Don't miss the compassion and empathy of Jesus here. Many commentators vary in their opinions on why Jesus wept. I think he wept because Mary and Martha wept. Jesus knew the ultimate outcome, that Lazarus would be raised from the dead. Nevertheless, he allowed himself to be moved by his friends' grief. Then he reminded them that this situation would not end in death but be used greatly to reveal the glory of God.

God has always been working in me. He has empathized with me and grieved with me. My life has never been designed to end in darkness— and I believe, without a doubt, he will use the pieces of my story to reveal his glory.

Practicing anchoring myself in Jesus and allowing him to restore the rooms of my heart has come with a long history of redefining.

For a long time I had a misunderstanding of *abundance*, which I defined as all my wants and needs being met the way I wanted them met. All my prayers answered exactly the way I had prayed and tied into a nice and neat tidy bow. Fixed. All my boxes and plans for my life, checked. The abundant life meant things like this: plenty of money in my bank account, marriage by a certain age, kids, a white picket fence, and a worry-free, stress-free life.

This thought process and theology resulted in me trying to create the life I loved with my own control—loving myself more rather than loving God more and dying to self. Now, don't get me wrong. I don't believe God calls us to live unfulfilled, miserable, or empty lives. Quite the opposite actually. Jesus said he came so we could experience an abundant life (John 10:10). But what does that mean?

I would like to propose a definition of abundance that can't be taken from us when outside circumstances change and shift. Some people define abundance as endless vacations. But God wants us to experience an inner life that we don't feel a need to escape. I believe soul abundance is a kingdom principle that comes from being rooted in the Spirit. Abundance is the fruit we bear in our lives when the way we live our lives is rooted in kingdom principles. This fruit is the satisfying food the world is seeking so hard after. We see people searching for significance and fame through clicks, likes, and fol-

God wants us to experience an inner life that we don't feel a need to escape.

lowers. We see people searching for worth and peace through money, achievements, and looks. But I have news: all the Botox and fillers in the world won't buy you worth.

Galatians 5:22–23 teaches us that true life and soul abundance looks like peace, joy, kindness, patience, and other fruits that only grow when you are rooted in Christ.

We are made to worship, and we are all worshipers, worshiping what we truly love, what satisfies us. We all become more like the thing we worship. Idols grow in the soil of our deepest wounds. They are the things we lean heavily on for satisfaction and worth outside of God when we're in pain, aware of our deficiencies. They might soften the pain in short spurts, but they cannot bring us lasting healing.

For a long time, even though I knew Jesus, I also searched (not always consciously) for other things to fill the gaping holes in my life. I tried filling those voids with *more*. More approval. More success. More security.

This is what Jesus was saying in John 4 to the woman he met at the well in Samaria. Every day she would go to the well, fill up her jars, and have to return again the next day, and the next, and the next. This is a picture of what we do when we seek to be filled up by our idols rather than Jesus. We will continue to return to wells that run dry. But Jesus says, "Whoever drinks of the water that I will give him will never be thirsty again" (v. 14). This abundance he offers is like living beside a natural spring that never dries up.

What well are you drawing from today?

After mere weeks of living here, I know there are no shortcuts to making this place beautiful, solid, and secure again. But I try. Oh, how I try.

A crack has opened up in one of the walls. I examine it and decide not to call a contractor. This is something I can handle myself. An easy fix. I caulk it, paint it, and bam! It's all fixed up. The crack is gone. My confidence grows.

A few days later, after a good, wet storm, I walk by that wall and spot a hairline fissure where the crack used to be. I'm on it fast: caulk, paint, voilà! Fixed.

A week later, the same.

A month later, again. That pesky crack keeps breaking through my work! It just keeps showing up. I'm getting tired of fixing this same issue over and over and over again. But what else can I do? I fetch the supplies and tools and get back at it.

After a few rounds of this, a contractor working on another area in my house sees my frustration. I sense him pause behind me while I concentrate. Maybe *this* time my work will hold.

"I wish you'd let me fix that for you," he says kindly.

The offer pricks a tiny bit of defensiveness in me. I can't deny it. What does he know about caulk and paint that I don't? This isn't brain surgery.

He points at the floor.

"Your issue is that your foundation is off right there. There's something shifting and moving at the base, and it's causing that crack to keep coming up. You need a true repair."

The foundation? Okay, maybe it *is* brain surgery.

Whatever it is, I catch his meaning right away. The truth of it hits me straight in the heart.

"I do want the help," I say. "I do want a true repair. Thank you."

The process is costly and messy—fixing a pier-and-beam foundation like the one I have is no simple task. But when the contractor is finished, I never have to deal with that crack again.

Jesus longs to be invited into the broken spaces of our lives. He longs to be our Master Carpenter, our Master Fixer, to care for our deepest needs and fill our needy spaces with himself. These rooms and parts of ourselves we want to hide from him or others are often the areas where he does his most miraculous, transformative work.

Jesus longs to be invited into the broken spaces of our lives.

One of my neediest spaces was the part of myself that had experienced feelings of abandonment. Jesus spoke to this wound directly when he said, "I will not leave you as orphans; I will come to you. . . . Because I live, you also will live" (John 14:18–19). These comforting words have sustained me through many dark nights. The truth is, I am not abandoned. Not by God.

Restoration is not something we can do ourselves. The real healing work takes skilled hands that know how to truly repair. Healing and growth take a long time, but in Christ we are assured they will happen. Jesus didn't come for the healthy but for the sick (Mark 2:17), because he alone has the remedy. He is our true foundation, the Rock that never moves. He never shifts or changes.

RESTORATION PRACTICE

Start Drawing from the Well of Jesus

Name your well or wells right now. Write them down. Write down the ways in which you've worked on filling that well, and then write about how you can draw from the well of Jesus instead. What does that look like? Does it look like letting go of something? Does it look like investing in yourself in a concrete way to fix a foundational issue?

As an additional option, consider asking a friend what *they* perceive as the wells they see you drawing from. Sometimes our dearest connections can see in us what is so hard to see in ourselves.

6

THE APPRENTICE

You Can Bind Yourself to God in the Waiting

I'm staring at Peggy like an alien just walked in.

The room we're sitting in is quaint. It's located in the corner office of a church she counsels out of a couple days a week. Every time I walk down the hallway and through this door, I feel a tension in my chest, a small tightening of a little fear and a lot of hope. There's a wooden desk and a couch in the room, and we always sit at the desk straight across from each other. We're only five minutes into our session and Peggy has already set out a box of tissues, as I need them often.

Most days I come in with a long list of things I want to talk about: my memories of the hard things that have happened and the people in my life that I feel are an unhealthy presence, causing me pain, tough circumstances, and so on. My mental folder is always organized and ready to go. I'm coming in hot with a lot of names and complaints about how they're affecting my life.

But today all that changed, as Peggy just looked me in the eyes and compassionately but firmly said to me, "Today we are going to talk about you, Meshali."

"Me?" I respond.

My stomach drops, and I fear the look on my face is as shocked and confused as I feel. How are we going to talk about me? And *why*, when I came prepared with my list? Is this a test?

"Yes," she says. "Today we are going to talk about your responsibility in your healing and your journey."

Mind you, Peggy has been walking with me in my journey for a while now through some extremely hard, deeply painful things. We've spent many sessions together talking about those things freely and without shame, because releasing those issues is a big key to my healing. The Lord has been digging up a lot that I've deeply buried. Counseling created a safe place for me to process that. Up to now, I had talked about what had happened and had acknowledged the offenses. But today is different.

"People often come in and think that if they could fix everyone around them, their lives would be much easier," Peggy says. "But the only person you can really tend to is you."

I'm sitting here kind of dumbfounded, wishing I knew what to say. Her words hit me in a tender spot as I realize I've unconsciously fallen into a victim mentality about certain areas of my life. The tears begin to prick my eyes as I try to name what I'm feeling right now: Defenseless. Helpless. A victim, if I'm being honest. Have I been waving the white flag of surrender to the wrong things?

Her words are a hard mirror for me to look in. Hot tears I can't hold back stream down my face as I say, "How? I feel powerless to some of this, like I just simply can't get better. Shame is holding me hostage. I won't ever be enough to be lovable. The things other people do will always get the better of me."

She invites me to close my eyes and walk away from those thoughts for a minute. "Envision yourself standing in a field of grass that's dying," she said. "You're holding a water hose. I want you to turn the hose down and water the grass that you're standing on. Water there first. The Lord wants to heal and strengthen you. He can do this despite others around you. No matter what they do, you can be whole and healed."

I suddenly feel so, so tired. The kind of tired that hits when you realize you've been working really hard and haven't accomplished anywhere near as much as you'd hoped. The kind of tired a house cleaner would feel after scrubbing a house top to bottom—and then realizing they're at the wrong address.

At the same time, I also feel relief. Peggy has named something I need that I couldn't put words to before now. I've been looking in the wrong place for my healing, bringing lists to her without understanding a fuller picture. I can't control the behavior of others. I can't exist in this place where I try to shore up my own resilience with my own strength.

I turn the water on me, and the green grass starts to grow at my feet.

Many passages in the Bible promise strength to the weary. You might recognize these verses from Isaiah 40. I've read this passage many times and heard it all my life. I've seen it displayed on coffee cups, home decor, stationery, you name it.

> Have you not known? Have you not heard?
> The Lord is the everlasting God,
>   the Creator of the ends of the earth.
> He does not faint or grow weary;
>   his understanding is unsearchable.
> He gives power to the faint,
>   and to him who has no might he increases strength.
> Even youths shall faint and be weary,
>   and young men shall fall exhausted;
> *but they who wait for the Lord shall renew their strength*;
>   they shall mount up with wings like eagles;
> they shall run and not be weary;
>   they shall walk and not faint. (vv. 28–31)

A few years back I was rereading this, and something jumped out at me. The Hebrew root of that word "wait" is *qavah* (pronounced kaw-vaw'). This word is an active verb that has nothing to do with hanging around doing nothing. At its heart, *qavah* is about expectation. I like to think of it as "waiting with purpose." A woman about to give birth waits for her baby in the *qavah* sense when she prepares the nursery. A person scrolling on their phone while standing in line at a Six Flags ride does not.

Qavah has an additional, deeper meaning: "to bind together (perhaps by twisting)."[1] If you like, you could read this verse as "they who bind

together with the Lord shall renew their strength." Other versions translate it as "hope in." The truth is that waiting is closely bound together with hope, and hope is closely bound together with waiting.

Healthy hope keeps us motivated. *Qavah* waits with expectation *and* action. Of course, what we put our hope in matters. Isaiah urges us to place it in the Lord, because if we bind ourselves together with the expectation of negative or horrible outcomes, we'll experience only anxiety and panic. So in a way, *qavah* means to entwine yourself with God, like tying yourself to him in a three-legged race.

Waiting is closely bound together with hope, and hope is closely bound together with waiting.

There's a similar idea in the New Testament. Jesus calls it "abiding."

> Abide in me, and I in you. As the branch cannot bear fruit by itself, unless it abides in the vine, neither can you, unless you abide in me. I am the vine; you are the branches. Whoever abides in me and I in him, he it is that bears much fruit, for apart from me you can do nothing. If anyone does not abide in me he is thrown away like a branch and withers; and the branches are gathered, thrown into the fire, and burned. If you abide in me, and my words abide in you, ask whatever you wish, and it will be done for you. By this my Father is glorified, that you bear much fruit and so prove to be my disciples. As the Father has loved me, so have I loved you. Abide in my love. (John 15:4–9)

These biblical concepts of waiting and abiding encourage us to remain in God, to tether ourselves tightly to him. We are the apprentice learning from the Master Carpenter as he moves through the house that is our life, repairing and renewing and refurbishing. The Master doesn't do the work for the apprentice. The Master patiently teaches the skills until the apprentice is trained. If we separate ourselves from him, what can we learn? What pain and frustration will we inflict on ourselves?

Paul uses the metaphor of gentiles being "grafted" into the vine of God's chosen people (Rom. 11:11–19), and this visual comes to mind when I read John 15. The process of grafting involves wrapping the vines together so tightly that what is separate grows together as one. When we abide and remain and tether ourselves to Jesus, we grow in our identity in him. We gain fresh perspective. We bear new fruit. We are strengthened.

In our waiting seasons we build strength for our soaring seasons.

Oftentimes we think of strength being in the soaring, but the truth is that in our waiting seasons we build strength *for* our soaring seasons. Those that *qavah* (wait and bind together) with the Lord shall renew their strength. They will mount up with wings as eagles. They will run but not grow weary, and walk but not faint.

What a promise.

We don't *qavah* to get anything and everything we want. We do it to connect with God through communion, prayer, and worship, and to depend on God as our provider and sustainer. Partnering with God in our restoration process is us doing what God has asked us to do—and trusting that he will do what only he can through *his* power in us.

My kitchen is a happy place, full of light. From the sink or stove I can catch views of the green yard and birds. My sister just bought me a new back door with windows, and a robin has recently taken an interest in the view from the outside in. He comes to perch on my screen door at dinnertime and peers through the panes of glass to watch me cook.

With all the work this house requires, I've had to renovate in stages and abide by a budget. Right now I can't do *everything* I want to in the room where I spend so much time throughout the day. I've put down new flooring, installed a simple tile backsplash and functioning appliances, painted the cabinets, and put up a few shelves. It's a vast improvement. But someday I'd like to make it more than functional. I dream of bigger, sturdier cabinets and trendy countertops, as well as a floor that's perfectly coordinated.

These are things I don't have the skills to do myself. I can paint. I can swing a sledgehammer and rip up a floor. But I don't know how to build new cabinets and hang them so they don't fall off the walls. I don't know how to hook up plumbing so the kitchen doesn't flood, or measure and cut heavy countertops that won't crack or crash through the floor. These skills are beyond me.

So for now, I wait. I water where I've been planted. I do what I can in the meantime.

Panic attacks have been an off-and-on battle for me during parts of my life. In the earliest days I didn't have that label for my experience. After all, I was a Christian kid in a ministry family in a conservative small town. Anxiety and mental health were taboo topics—or signs of a weak faith. I remember hiding my feelings, because if anyone knew, they'd think badly of me.

The beginning of my battle with anxiety was also the beginning of my habit of hiding and performing. If I could just be great at everything I put my hands to, if I could just excel, the panic would stop, right? I would be valued and that would make me feel worthy. Boy was I shocked when the more I tried to make it okay, to *be* okay, the worse the attacks got.

I tried harder. The performance habit seeped into my faith journey. Just as I tried to work my way into people being pleased with me, I tried to work my way into God being pleased with me. I had no idea God didn't require this of me.

When I was fourteen, a connection happened I couldn't have foreseen. I was invited to share at my youth group for the first time. I was excited and honored, and I was also very nervous. I adored my youth pastors, and the church I attended was home to me. I loved this second family of mine, this chosen family that did a lot of life together—and not only on Sundays. They put a high value on good speakers and ministers who were truly anointed. I didn't realize how much was being wired and crossed in my brain.

My youth group had about fifty kids, and I might as well have been prepping for the Super Bowl. I outlined my message, prayed, wrote it down, read through it, and practiced reciting it until I was good to go.

The big day rolled around, and a nervous pit in the bottom of my stomach sat there all day long. I was so hyperfixated on the night, I probably barely said two words to my friends at school that day. So many stopped to say things like, "We can't wait to hear you tonight, Meshali! We know it's going to be great and powerful!"

The evening service rolled around, and I got up behind the podium to speak. I greeted my peers. I looked around and noticed my youth pastors smiling at me and saw precious faces I loved in the crowd. My heart beat so loud in my ears I couldn't hear. The room was shaking and spinning as I tried to calm myself. I felt woozy and weak. All I could hear was this tape that played on a loop in my head: "You have to do this right, Meshali . . . Don't get this wrong . . . There's no room for error . . . Lots of people came to hear you, and they're counting on you. Your pastors are listening. Your friends are listening . . . You can't let anyone down . . . You need to speak . . . You need to be the BEST."

I shared that I'd be speaking about the prodigal son, and then words failed me. The pressure to perform kicked into high gear and raced out of my mind and straight into my body. The room closed in on me until the blackness took over all my sight.

And then I was waking up. On the floor.

I had passed out right there in front of everyone.

Now, being in a Pentecostal church, some thought I had fallen under the power of the Lord. Today this makes me laugh. But at the time I was confused. I felt shame, even though no one around me was making a fuss and there were a ton of people at the altar. A lot of people were saved that night, but I don't remember the service at all.

I left and had no tools to process my experience, so I buried it. My young brain attached that panic to the stage and to the experience of public speaking. From then on, I wrestled with intense anxiety every single time I got up to share at a church.

This is an anxiety that still tries to fight me at times, one that I've noticed tends to get worse if I avoid it. So now I bring it out into the light, I name it, and its power over me begins to wane. This hasn't released me and made me fully free of worry about what people think of me on a stage, but because I am learning how to *qavah*—how to bind myself to the security of God while I wait for my ultimate healing—it has allowed me to take a breath and fight the urge to let the panic take over.

Every time I separate myself from the tape of lies and expectations that plays in my mind and instead abide in the truth of God's Word, the grip of anxiety weakens and his strength in me grows. "For God has not given us a spirit of fear, but of power and of love and of a sound mind" (2 Tim. 1:7 NKJV). Fear, which keeps me small, peels off me in the presence of God, who invites me daily to take my seat at the table—a seat I haven't earned for any reason. I can rest with a sound mind in knowing that he loves me and I am bound to his love.

I wake feeling a bit sideways, off-balance for no reason I'm able to name. As I lie in bed and look around me to get my bearings, things just feel oddly *heavy*. My mind is suddenly filled with some of the things in my heart I'm waiting on in this season—some unfulfilled hopes. Some expectations. Here they are again, at the forefront of my mind, clamoring for my attention. They make me feel lonely and a little fearful. I'm a morning person who usually shoots out of bed. But today I'm tossing and turning in bed before I feel I can rise, consumed by these niggling thoughts.

As much as I love my life and celebrate all of God's goodness and beauty in it, some days my heart still aches for things I hope and wait for. This is some of the tension of *qavah* and restoration. Last year there was an industry-wide shortage of roofing shingles, and my friend who needed a new roof waited six months before it could be installed. Would materials come before winter hit? How would the damaged roof hold up under the next storm? Waiting was the only solution. Worry accomplished nothing, but it was hard not to think about that roof and when it would be set to rights.

When I'm tired—physically, emotionally, or mentally—things tend to feel bigger than they really are, more urgent and awful. My

questions and doubts seem to scream at me a little louder or bother me a bit more.

About an hour goes by and I'm still in bed. It hits me that I'm lying here ruminating on my problems and what I think I lack instead of focusing on gratitude and praise to God for all the beautiful blessings he's given me. I think about the mirror Peggy held up to me.

Don't fixate on the dry grass, Meshali. Water it.

It turns out God is not the parent who's still cutting our food into small bites even though we're adults. In the practice of *qavah*, there's work for us to do.

Deep breath, Meshali.

The day stretches ahead of me, and I know it's up to me how I'll think about it and face it. I finally rise and sit down at the kitchen table, close my eyes, and bind myself to Jesus. I begin to thank the Lord for who he is. I begin to thank him for life and blessings, visualizing specific ones, specific people and opportunities. My home, the breath in my lungs, a car to drive. Fresh coffee. I thank God for the gift of friendships. The gift of Jesus. I spend time in prayer and thanksgiving and turn on some worship music.

Today, I'm choosing to do as Paul advises: "Whatever is true, whatever is honorable, whatever is just, whatever is pure, whatever is lovely, whatever is commendable, if there is any excellence, if there is anything worthy of praise, think about these things" (Phil. 4:8).

And then the desires in my heart no longer matter—they simply disappear . . .

Just kidding.

But now these yearnings and hopes and dreams are tied to God. Now I can *qavah*.

Lest you think that is the only time I've done that, or that this is a one-time process, let me encourage you from someone who has been there and is there. I am always working toward this, always handing it to God, always working to water the ground at my feet.

Watering this dry grass below us, turning our thoughts to what is lovely and excellent, is no dismissal of our desires or needs. *Qavah* does not erase our hopes with sickly sweet optimism, it merely waits on God's perfect timing and instruction, aware that God knows our longings and worries and cares about it all. He longs to give us good gifts. Jesus said,

> Ask, and it will be given to you; seek, and you will find; knock, and it will be opened to you. For everyone who asks receives, and the one who seeks finds, and to the one who knocks it will be opened. Or which one of you, if his son asks him for bread, will give him a stone? Or if he asks for a fish, will give him a serpent? If you then, who are evil, know how to give good gifts to your children, how much more will your Father who is in heaven give good things to those who ask him! (Matt. 7:7–11)

Qavah gives us a way to steward our desires and expectations by submitting them to the God of love. God wants our hearts, to be close to us. He wants us to bring these prayers and petitions to him in a posture of hope and surrender.

God is not a vending machine. He is not at our beck and call, granting every single request with the push of a button. But he is a loving Father who sees all, knows best, and is working *all* things together for our good and his glory (Rom. 8:28). He deeply cares about our waiting. He deeply cares about us in the process.

Our responsibility is to surrender by abiding in him, to celebrate all God has done in our lives while we also look to the future in hope and expectation.

We can bind our lives to God the way a baby is bound to its mama in a sling or papoose—being carried everywhere, responsible for nothing, crying when we're needy. Or we can bind our lives to God as if he is a genie we carry in our water bottle, pulling him out whenever we need something. But I'd like to propose—from personal experience and also learning the hard way—a more life-giving way of waiting in these stagnant seasons of life. We can bind our lives to God as if we're in a three-legged race, running together, each doing our part. We move, stop, pivot with God. We tether ourselves to

God deeply cares about our waiting.

him and place all our weight upon him, a stable force in an unstable world.

In the next section of this book, I'll share the practices that have helped to stabilize and strengthen my own life in this season of *qavah*.

All life is found in God. Every treasure we could ever desire is in him. The true treasure of life is knowing that in the midst of whatever is going on in our lives, God is *with* us, Immanuel, at every single phase of our restoration process. What the enemy means for evil, God uses for his glory. And we get to partner with him, learn from him, lean into him, grow in him, and see him with our own eyes.

In beholding God, we can't help but change and grow.

RESTORATION PRACTICE

Bind Yourself to God

Where have you placed your hope? To what—to whom—have you bound yourself? Do you bind yourself to God like a helpless baby, a wishful soul, or an apprentice, a partner in a three-legged race? Consider the metaphor that really captures the heart of *qavah* and helps you think clearly about this way of living. Write down one thing you can start doing today to keep yourself tightly bound to God in this season of waiting on him with hopeful expectation.

PART 3

RENEWAL

7

REBUILDING ON SOLID ROCK

Christ Is Your Firm Foundation

My brother Trey is running beside me, sharing his heart with me in panting breaths as our feet pound the pavement. He asks me how I am and, as always, tells me I'm beautiful. I decide to open up to him a door I've tried to hide behind—my never-ending battle with how I see myself. That I struggle to believe it's genuine when someone—anyone—tells me I'm beautiful.

He stops dead in his tracks.

Sweat drips down his face, like mine, and he looks as serious as I've ever seen him. "Meshali, I love you and you're beautiful. But it doesn't matter what others think. I want YOU to know that and see that." He leans down and puts his hands on his knees, takes a deep breath, and looks at me. I know he's serious by the way he holds his head up and the look in his eyes. "If I have to call you every day from here on out to remind you of that, I will."

I know he means it, and it makes me feel loved and seen. I also know that it's not healthy or sustainable if he has to call me every day to remind me of this. But I feel he's onto something. This particular pain in my heart has felt like a red flag for a while now, filling me with a new knowing that God needs to mend something here. Image has become my identity in the last few years, and I can see now that it's become one of the faulty foundations I've attempted building my life on.

As each day goes on, I've noticed I can be feeling good, and then in a moment—maybe with one person saying the wrong thing to me at the wrong time—*boom*. There was that crack. Triggered again. It never fails to send me into a downward spiral of negative thoughts about myself, my worth, even my future. Another tape on loop in my mind that tells me lies and serves up shame. It's time to stop the replay, and I know in my gut that inviting Trey into this hidden place of mine today is my first real footstep forward.

For any home, a solid foundation is crucial to *everything* about the home. The foundation gives a structure stability, bears weight, and prevents it from uneven settling and damage. It protects a home's structural integrity. And it helps the building to withstand life's forces—earthquakes, high winds, shifting soil, rushing waters—so that it's durable and safe.

Remember the wall in my home that kept cracking even after I'd "repaired" it repeatedly with my caulk? We can't live our lives with that quick fix, with the shortcuts that aren't real, foundational work.

We set our lives on faulty foundations or idols that cannot bear the weight of life, and then we crack when they fail us. And we crumble. When we face a crisis in life, it shows us where our foundation truly is. We must ask ourselves—where is our true strength and where does it come from?

If I know anything about life, it's that the storms are going to come. Jesus said that in Scripture (John 16:33). Our lives will be shaken, and only things of the kingdom will be unshakable. You might be familiar with the story Jesus told of the wise man:

> Everyone then who hears these words of mine and does them will be like a wise man who built his house on the rock. And the rain fell, and the floods came, and the winds blew and beat on that house, but it did not fall, because it had been founded on the rock. And everyone who hears these words of mine and does not do them will be like a foolish man who built his house on the sand. And the rain fell, and the floods came, and the winds blew and beat against that house, and it fell, and great was the fall of it. (Matt. 7:24–27)

Jesus emphasized not just hearing but *doing*. He says that the person who hears his words *and* demonstrates faith by acting on them is a wise builder. James echoed this truth when he wrote in James 2:17 that faith without works (action) is dead (worthless).

This kind of hearing and doing requires faith. To be faithful to something or someone is to be loyal—dedicated, devoted, steadfast, constant, and full of confident assurance in the object of our faith. When we have faith in God, we put our hope and trust in life's only solid foundation. "You are God's building," Paul wrote. "Because of God's grace to me, I have laid the foundation like an expert builder. Now others are building on it. But whoever is building on this foundation must be very careful. For no one can lay any foundation other than the one we already have—Jesus Christ" (1 Cor. 3:9–11 NLT).

When we have faith in God, we put our hope and trust in life's only solid foundation.

And so we read the Word of God, applying it to every area of our lives, and put its truths into practice. This is something we have to do, something we must incorporate into the daily rhythms of our lives. God won't do it for us. For many years, I wanted transformation without spiritual formation. In other words, I wanted God to do a miracle in my life (*Fix me, please! Take this feeling away from me, please!*) that didn't require any effort on my part. But spiritual formation—a critical part of our restoration—only happens when we take initiative and engage.

There was a time in my life when the body dysmorphia I dealt with was severe. I hated my body. What I thought I saw in the mirror was completely different from reality. I was in search of something, anything, to make me feel valuable. In my mind, I began to believe perfection in my body and image would achieve this. Maybe if I could ever be skinny enough, look good enough, I would find the balm my soul needed. Find relief from this ache. Feel worthy.

I love to run and would regularly turn on a podcast or music and take off. But this hobby I loved, a healthy outlet, soon became something that began to drive *me*. I would get out and find myself running and running . . . and running. I would run until after dark, worrying my family. They started asking me if I was okay.

"Meshali, you've been out running for *hours*." I hadn't really noticed the time.

I would laugh and shrug it off, but I knew privately what my motivation was: to get in a few more minutes and burn a few more calories. I drew no boundary lines around my exercise. I became consumed with constantly thinking about what I was eating, calculating how many calories I was taking in versus burning. And no matter how I looked, I was never small enough in my own eyes.

The drive to be "acceptable" grew to be a monster in my mind. I was hardly able to look at myself in photos, and when I did, I saw nothing beautiful. This mindset robbed me of joy, of life. I was building my life on the foundation of my image, which was never good enough. Nothing was enough. The bar I'd set was too high, unattainable, creating a cycle of misery. Instead of being founded on Christ and the high price he paid for me, instead of my value and worth being secure and unshakable in him, I could only try harder and harder to depend on myself—on what I could produce, on my image. Vanity.

I'll repeat myself: Our idols grow in the soil of our wounds. Image was my idol, and I was willing to do whatever it took to keep up appearances. I was drowning in the opinions of others. No matter how much encouragement I got from people close to me, it never seemed to penetrate my heart or be enough.

Even back then, I knew on the surface that I was fearfully and wonderfully made in the image of God (Ps. 139:14), but I needed that truth to make its way from my head down into my heart. I needed to hear it, apply the Word, know it, really believe it. I began to ask Jesus to help me. Making this change took a disciplined practice of choosing to believe God's truth over my own mind's messages several times a day—sometimes hourly, sometimes minute by minute—until my heart began to really believe it was true. When we intentionally renew our mind in Christ, we're changed from the inside out.

Picking up the pieces and rebuilding my identity on the foundation of God and his Word has taken time. The lesson I learned about vanity and image has crept up again in other areas of my life. In certain seasons I've found myself building on other foundations that also aren't about my true value in Christ: my career, my relationships, my possessions. Of course, when you build your identity on these things, you have to keep them up, which requires perfectionism and constant work.

When Christ is our foundation, the work requires less effort. We're not trying to manage our life with the limited strength of our own skills. We have the unlimited strength of Christ when we abide in him. Jesus told his disciples: "If you keep my commandments, you will abide in my love, just as I have kept my Father's commandments and abide in his love. These things I have spoken to you, that my joy may be in you, and that your joy may be full" (John 15:10–11).

Without Jesus we can do nothing that matters and build nothing that lasts. Nothing that will endure the storms of life. Only by abiding in Christ can our joy be made full.

For me, abiding in Christ has come to mean not only hearing what he says and believing it but also doing it, obeying his Word. This means developing certain spiritual practices that keep me firmly on the foundation that is Jesus: discipline, repentance, forgiveness, and surrender.

> *Only by abiding in Christ can our joy be made full.*

Every single one of these practices is harder to do on some days than others, but the more I stick with it, the more habitual they become.

Discipline isn't really a feel-good word, especially in our culture today. Discipline is about developing consistent, habitual behaviors. Through such practice, a disciplined person submits to training to gain mastery over themselves, their thoughts, and their actions. They will forgo doing what's easy if doing what's difficult is the better choice. They are open to the type of training that corrects, shapes, and perfects their mental state and moral character. They are self-controlled and obedient to their guiding principles.

As much as discipline is a hard word and even harder practice, I firmly believe it's a pathway to some of the best fruit of your life. If you lift weights regularly, you'll build muscle. If you practice memorizing God's Word, it will come to mind whenever you need it. If you guard your relationship with God, you'll never drift away. Discipline is a road that leads to health, wholeness, balance, and good boundaries.

When it came to my body dysmorphia, I chose to follow Paul's disciplinary advice to "destroy arguments and every lofty opinion raised against the knowledge of God, and take every thought captive to obey Christ" (2 Cor. 10:5). Day after day after day I had to *decide* to believe what God said about me, even over what my own mind was trying to tell me. And little by little it became easier to do.

Repentance is a word we usually think of in terms of turning away from sin and correcting our behavior, dedicating ourselves to being or doing better. And that's an important facet of the change that repentance brings about. We have to crucify the things that would separate us from God and replace those with thoughts and behaviors that bring life to the world. Like discipline, this isn't easy work, but it is important work.

Another interpretation of repentance is "a change of mind." Jesus challenged his followers to think about the world in an upside-down way. He wasn't interested in the "whitewashed tombs" of religiosity. Instead he urged people to have radically new views of inclusion, service, wealth, power, and love. I had to change my mind about the farmhouse being too much work to be troubled with. I had to change my mind about the truth of my body and my self-worth. I had to change my mind about whether God had abandoned me or was doing a good work in my life even when I couldn't see it.

When I finally covered the walls with fresh coats of Alabaster White paint, I knew they didn't just look clean, they *were* clean.

Forgiveness, to me, is about entrusting to God the wounds that others inflict on us. I once heard a story about a boy who caught a lizard in his yard. It bit him on the hand, but he was so focused on the fact of having caught the thing that he kept his grip on the wriggly reptile while he ran crying to his dad. "Put it down so I can look at the bite," his dad said. But the boy wouldn't let go of his catch. It bit him again and again. He just couldn't let go, caught between feeling hurt and scared and wanting to hold on to the very thing causing him pain.

God is like that dad begging his son to put down the lizard so he can take care of things. Can you trust him to understand the problem and tend your wounds? There's only so much he can do until we decide to let go.

I've had to forgive quite a few people over my lifetime for offenses ranging from traumatic abuse to cutting me off in traffic. Some lizards are easy to let go of. Others, for whatever reason, stay in the death grip of my closed fist far longer than is necessary. Sometimes I put the lizard of my offense down and then pick it up again. Why do we hold on? For some of us, our pain is our identity. Some of us just don't know how to let go. And if we're honest with ourselves, some of us want justice more than we want healing. Some of us think forgiveness lets offenders walk free. In truth, it sets *us* free.

> *Some of us think forgiveness lets offenders walk free. In truth, it sets us free.*

I was one of those people who simply didn't know how to forgive. I began learning by asking the Lord to help me. One morning I lay on the living room floor, praying for help, desperately wanting to be free from the pain of a deep, difficult offense. I was raised on old church hymns and songs and have such an affection for them. A song from my childhood, "Oh the Glory of His Presence," came on the TV. I told God I was so tired of hanging on to unforgiveness. I wanted to lay it down, but I felt like I couldn't in my own power. I felt the Lord's compassion rush over me. Tears streamed down my cheeks, and I began to meditate on how much I myself have been forgiven. I've not only been forgiven but I've been restored much more than I deserve.

As I began to ruminate on the forgiveness God has extended toward me, I began to ask the Lord to help me extend that same grace to one of the people in my life who had hurt me the deepest. This is how I began to forgive: wanting to, choosing to, seeing my own shortcomings, accepting

Christ's forgiveness, and then extending that forgiveness to others. It was a profound moment but also merely the beginning of a process.

For a long time I had walked with invisible chains keeping me bound to the ones who hurt me most. These chains dictated how I saw the world, how I felt, how I functioned. But when I forgave and cut the chains, that power began to lose its grip on me. I even began to feel and experience compassion for the offenders.

God wants to free us from the prison cell where we sit nursing the wounds from every wrong ever done to us, whether we broadcast our pain or not. Forgiveness happens in the secret, hidden places of our heart. If your heart is locked up in a prison of offense, forgiveness is your key to freedom.

Surrender and forgiveness go hand in hand. When we surrender our offenses to God, we give up a *thing*. But he is capable of caring for even more than the wrongs done to us. He would like us to give up claim to our whole life. He's the Great Architect who knows what's best for us in any situation. A surrendered life isn't stagnant or lazy, it's trusting. We work with him not to get the life we dreamed of but the life he would like to give to us.

Surrender is Jesus praying "not my will, but yours" in Gethsemane (Luke 22:42). Surrender is trusting his plan even when our plans fall apart. Surrender is the opposite of control. And like discipline, repentance, and forgiveness, surrender isn't a one-and-done event but a way of life.

I don't run for hours anymore. In fact, sometimes my runs are punctuated with text conversations. Today I'm running past some beautiful oak trees, and a friend and I are chatting about faithfulness, a word most of us don't talk about much. A talk bubble pops up on my screen as I see my friend writing a message back to me.

"You know," they write, "the oak tree is already in the acorn."

This sticks with me as I make my way home. They're talking about the fruits of a faithful life. These huge, magnificent trees of such incredible strength are already present in the tiny acorn. It emerges slowly, over a long time, responding to regular tending with the essentials: water, soil, and sunshine.

I think about that as I approach my farmhouse. So many of these foundational practices are rooted in our commitment to them on easy and hard days alike. For a really long time, I let my feelings dictate how my days would go and which practices I would keep up. This was a huge problem because feelings will always ebb and flow. I know now that if I stay consistent, I will see the fruit. My breaths steady as my steps slow, and I'm home again.

With all of life's demands, it's important to pause daily and evaluate the strength of your life's foundation. Any good apprentice takes their time and devotes extra care to their work. We have to stop and do the same, praying with the psalmist, "Search me, O God, and know my heart; try me and know my anxious thoughts; and see if there be any hurtful way in me, and lead me in the everlasting way" (Ps. 139:23–24 NASB).

I want you to hear me cheering you on, and I also want you to keep your focus on the lasting fruit that discipline, repentance, forgiveness, and surrender will produce in your life. Many times these practices will go against the flow of our human nature and will feel like something we don't necessarily want to do. This is where we feel the war of the flesh. But through our obedience and the help of the Holy Spirit's grace, we can plant, water, and tend to our growth. Soon we'll see the fruit.

RESTORATION PRACTICE

Shore Up the Foundation of Your Faith

Where are the cracks in your foundation? Take an inventory of the practices in this chapter and honestly assess the attention you give these:

	Never				Always
Reading God's Word	1	2	3	4	5
Believing God's Word	1	2	3	4	5
Obeying God's Word	1	2	3	4	5
Practicing Discipline	1	2	3	4	5
Practicing Repentance	1	2	3	4	5
Practicing Forgiveness	1	2	3	4	5
Practicing Surrender	1	2	3	4	5

I am not grading you, and no one is judging you. This is an inventory for *you*. A muscle that is exercised gets stronger over time. Which of these spiritual muscles could be strengthened? Pick just one to start with and consciously add it to your day until it becomes a habit. When you are ready, add and strengthen another, and so on.

8

THE LOAD-BEARING BEAMS OF SOUL CARE

You Will Find Rest for Your Soul

At the moment, the living room fireplace is cold. The space is dark and small. It would be hard for many of my friends and family members to comfortably gather in here. But it's one of my favorite rooms because I can see in my mind's eye everything the space will be by the time we're finished with this particular restoration project: an open floor plan full of light, a flowing space, a crackling fire, and a full dining room table visible from the roomy sofa. I see a place for everyone to sit and share stories, eat together, laugh, and do life. I've been thinking about this since the first time I saw the house. The possibilities thrill me, and I figure the solution is pretty simple.

"This wall is in the way," I say to the contractor standing beside me. "It's blocking a lot of light, and it makes the floor plan choppy. Everything will feel bigger and more connected if we take it down. I'll help swing the sledgehammer!"

I expect him to agree. People take down walls all the time, right? Besides, these days there's nothing a good contractor can't do. I watch HGTV.

He doesn't share my excitement. "That'll be a big job, Meshali."

"Why?"

"Well, that's a load-bearing wall you're wanting to knock out. All the load-bearing walls have to be secure for the house to stand correctly."

My heart sinks like the roofline over the front porch—I know immediately what he's talking about. The load-bearing beam at the front of the house has weakened over the years and begun to droop. The dip in the middle is visible from the road. We're going to have to replace the sagging beam and reframe the front of the house. But that's outside. In here, am I asking for the impossible?

He assures me I'm not, but I need to put my sledgehammer down for a while. "We'll need to secure a new beam to hold the load before we can take down the wall. The load-bearing beam is vital. It has to be done right or else . . ."

He doesn't have to explain. A terrible vision of my home collapsing from the center outward comes easily enough.

Load-bearing beams work in tandem with a properly laid foundation. They bear the weight of floors and roofs, distributing weight evenly and transferring it to the ground. They save walls and windows from sagging like a melting candle. They also make it possible to have an open floor plan with fewer walls and more light. I can't think of a better metaphor for the kind of bright and open life I want to lead.

Support beams aren't always visible. They often hide behind sheetrock or siding. When our life is broken, we may think the answer to our problems is outside ourselves or requires a change in external circumstances, but often the answer is found in the inner work. There is a tending that needs to happen at the soul level.

Soul is one of those words we use a lot without real clarity about what it is. I love John Ortberg's definition: "What is running your life at any given moment is your soul. Not external circumstances, not your thoughts, not your intentions, not even your feelings, but your soul. The soul is that aspect of your whole being that correlates, integrates and enlivens everything going on in the various dimensions of the self. The soul is the life center of human beings."[1]

The life center. What is running your life at any given moment.

Your soul might be the most important thing about you. We're sometimes quick to neglect the soul because we can't see it, touch it, weigh it, or measure it. When life is full, we might forget it completely. But rest assured, whether we're paying attention to it or not, our soul is running our life. Like those load-bearing beams, the soul is vital to who we are and what we do. It supports everything. And if it's in disrepair, our lives will eventually collapse.

I hate that pain and brokenness impact us all. But living in this fallen world, we humans cannot escape that reality. We experience heartbreak, injustice, trauma, pain, damage to our souls. But Jesus cares about this part of us too. He bears the weight where we are weak and invites us into a strengthening partnership with him. He fortifies the beams of our lives and gives us a vision for what can be. We don't have to go back to life as it was so long as we practice the disciplines that keep our inner beams strong.

> *Whether we're paying attention to it or not, our soul is running our life. Like those load-bearing beams, the soul is vital to who we are and what we do.*

One night several years back, I lay down in bed and set my alarm for 2:30 a.m., when I'd need to get up for a flight out of DFW to New York City. I had to be at the airport to check in with my gear and luggage by 4:00. It was my third trip in the past week, and it seemed like I'd been shooting and traveling nonstop. I was up to my ears with edits and deadlines. I could feel my body breaking down under the weight of a busy schedule and the pressure to produce. And to produce perfectly, if possible.

My business was growing like crazy, and I was so grateful for that, but I was on the go constantly and not getting much sleep. My business model allowed everyone constant access to me. I regularly received texts from clients late into the night asking if their images could be ready sooner than our agreed-upon deadline. I had no clear sense of how many shoots I could realistically do each month. I was running hard with no boundaries or structure. And once I got started running, I was like a machine, and it was hard to know when to come to a halt.

I needed a pivot, a reset. I needed to stop long enough to take a real evaluation of my life—the frequency and demand of my schedule, my business hours, and what all the busyness and pressure was doing to my soul. It was time to learn the rhythms and habits that worked for me in a healthy way.

When I was a teenager, I owned a really cool white Jeep Cherokee. It was stripped down, just the basics—upholstered seats, AM/FM radio—but it had everything I needed and I loved it. My friends and I would cruise our hometown avenue in that Jeep.

One summer, a light started flashing on the dash. I ignored it. I figured it would just go away if I left it alone long enough. I continued to drive the Jeep all over town, rushing around, loading it down with my friends and all the fun—until one day I got in and it wouldn't start. The Jeep simply wouldn't run anymore.

We had a local mechanic haul it to the shop. I told him about the light that had been flashing on and off for a while by then. He diagnosed the multiple problems and said, "You should have brought it in as soon as you started seeing that light. I could have fixed you right up. Ignoring the light may be what caused the worse problems."

I got better at recognizing warning lights after that. And not just the bright yellow kind. My body is good at flagging problems before they're real crises: fatigue, run-down immune system, aches and pains, crankiness. When the warning lights come on, I need to stop, evaluate the issue, and repair what's broken. It's so vital that we listen to what our soul is trying to tell us. When our bodies feel exhausted, when we feel overwhelmed in life, when we feel anxious or troubled but we continue to push through, we might be causing further damage to our inner lives and maybe even to the people around us.

Car maintenance is important—regularly changing the oil, looking under the hood, and making sure all fluids are topped off prevents damage to the engine. The same principle applies to our souls. Here are some "soul warning lights" that I try to take note of:

- Feeling anxious and not being able to get on top of it or name it
- Feeling overwhelmed
- Getting agitated easily
- Feeling tired all the time and not being able to catch up on rest

- Being worried about pleasing others
- Having an overcommitted calendar
- Lacking joy
- Lacking peace

Just because we have a full schedule doesn't mean we're living the abundant life. I've heard the saying "healthy things grow," and that's true, but so does cancer. As Christ followers, we are not owners of our own bodies but stewards of them. First Corinthians 3:16 says, "Do you not know that you are God's temple and that God's Spirit dwells in you?" For a long time I was moving at a pace that surpassed my ability to steward my temple well.

Tending to this is vital to living in abundance. Third John 1:2 says, "Beloved, I pray that all may go well with you and that you may be in good health, as it goes well with your soul." Another version says "as your soul prospers" (NASB). Taking care of ourselves spiritually, emotionally, and physically is vital to support the restoration of our lives. If one of these parts of us suffers, it affects everything else.

Spiritual Health

The practices that support our faith—discipline, repentance, forgiveness, and surrender—also support our overall spiritual wellness. Tending to our lives spiritually is our most vital act—the wellspring from which all else flows.

As we develop a strong faith that places obedience to God's Word at the center of our lives, the following regular practices support the ongoing health of our spirits:

- Commit to time in Bible study in order to learn and marinate in God's Word, allowing it to transform us.
- Commune with God through prayer, not only talking to God and offering praises, laments, and requests, but also listening to the still small voice he uses to speak to us.

- Honor the Sabbath day by allowing body and mind to rest, entrusting our resources and efforts to God. The weight of the world is not on us, even if we feel like it is. Our resting puts our trust in God on display. We know God's power can fill the gaps, and he can do more when we step aside to allow him to work.

Tending to our lives spiritually is our most vital act—the wellspring from which all else flows.

- Slow down. Even while we work, God repeatedly invites us to keep our attention on him, but we can't do this when we're focused only on rushing around from task to task or crisis to crisis. We can honestly evaluate whether we're too overextended to make room for God to be present in each moment.

- Guard our hearts against the flood of inputs—doomscrolling, unedifying entertainment, gossip and dissension, information overload, marketing and influencer ploys, and anything else that clamors for our attention—by separating ourselves from the distraction of technology at regular intervals.

- Root ourselves in community with other spiritually healthy people, whether that's a church body, a Bible study group, or another fellowship group or ministry.

Emotional Health

Some Christians are distrustful of emotions, believing they are unreliable or always lead us astray. But I think our emotions—positive and negative—are gifted to us by God, and I tend to agree with Dan Allender and Tremper Longman, who write, "Ignoring our emotions is turning our back on reality. Listening to our emotions ushers us into reality. And reality is where we meet God. . . . Emotions are the language of the soul."[2]

Negative emotions are part of our warning-light system. Fear, anger, sadness, anxiety, disgust, despair, and so on can make us uncomfortable or cause us to feel unacceptable. We can turn our back on them or allow them to tell us the truth: We have something important to surrender to God.

In my own journey, spiritual health and emotional health are connected. We can trust God with any feeling, no matter how complex it is. If you're in a season of emotional struggle, it doesn't mean you're spiritually lacking or something is wrong with you. How you're feeling is *important* to God. And bringing these emotions to God is vital to becoming healthy.

There are specific ways we can practice bringing our emotions to the Lord:

- Cry out to God through prayer. There is nothing we can't say to him. He is not bothered by our humanity. Jesus sympathizes with all our struggles and pain (Heb. 4:14–16).

- Read and pray the Psalms. Speak them aloud. The psalmists' words are full of deep, authentic emotion.

- Write a lament (see the Restoration Practice at the end of chapter 1).

- Keep a handwritten journal of the emotions you pour out to God. (Fun fact: Writing by hand might support brain health— and, by connection, emotional health—to a greater degree than typing.[3]) Document positive emotions too!

- Consult a counselor or therapist who supports biblical faith. The best therapists don't judge emotions but validate them. They can guide us into healthful ways of honoring and processing our emotions. A good therapist can also show us how to establish the kinds of healthy emotional boundaries that protect our hearts without hiding them behind impenetrable walls.

- Entrust emotions to reliable friends who will empathize but aren't willing to wallow with us in unhealthy places. We can surround ourselves with people who are kind and patient but unwilling to let us get stuck.

- Celebrate the full spectrum of human emotions. *Atlas of the Heart* by Brené Brown is a terrific resource for learning how to name specific feelings.

- Spend time on activities we enjoy but that don't place any demands on us. In other words, activities that are "just for fun."

- Spend time with people who bring us joy and support our well-being.

Physical Health

During the season when my load-bearing beams were starting to sag, I discovered a paradox: The more I needed support, the lazier I became with my daily healthy habits. The more I had on my plate, the more tired I felt, and the more I started to take shortcuts that undermined my health. It was as if I had ignored my contractor and started to swing that sledgehammer at the walls of my life when the beams were at their weakest. I'd grab fast food more often than nourishing my body with home-cooked, healthy meals. My pendulum swung from exercising for hours a day to exercising hardly at all. (Extreme exercise is unhealthy in its own way, but I had developed a reasonable habit that suffered.) Rather than getting enough sleep and Sabbath rest, I stayed up later, got up earlier, and often worked through weekends. I drank more caffeine than water. I'd driven my body to physical illness.

Even though physical health is the last item on this warning-lights list, it might be the most important one—kind of like a car's "check engine" light. When that one comes up, we don't want to mess around. The limitations of our bodies are real. I sometimes think about how Jesus met people's physical needs before meeting their spiritual needs. If they were hungry, he fed them. If they were sick, he healed them. If they had demons, he cast them out. If they were outcasts, he touched them. *Then* he commended their faith or gave them instructions or made a point of a spiritual teaching.

We live in a culture and an era where exhaustion seems to be a badge of honor. Being run-down because we are so busy earns us a lot of sympathy and praise. But at what cost?

Firmly securing the load-bearing beam of my physical health has been vital to my spiritual and emotional health. Though the specific details of a healthy life might vary from person to person, we can keep these practices in mind:

- Get enough sleep. We know when we're cheating ourselves. If you struggle with wakefulness in bed, my heart goes out to you! Learn about good sleep hygiene, supportive nutrition, and emotional and spiritual supports that might help. Don't give up.
- Move the body regularly throughout the day and in varied ways that are enjoyable. Include activities that support strength training, flexibility, and cardiovascular health.
- Listen to the body's pain signals and consult an expert to get to the root of the problems. Exercise adaptively when needed to accommodate limitations and healing.
- Ask a healthcare provider if any medications could be reduced or eliminated with lifestyle changes. I thank God we have pharmaceutical aids when we need them! But sometimes we rely on chemicals when we don't have to and at a cost to our bodies.
- Eat the best quality whole foods that fit the budget. Limit processed foods and added sugars as much as possible.
- Support nutrition with high-quality supplements where needed. A physician who practices functional or integrative medicine can help to identify these needs.
- Drink more water than other beverages.
- Limit time on screens as a rule, but especially during times dedicated to sleep, God, and interacting face-to-face with other people.

Slowing down to care for ourselves is a countercultural move. For a long time, I sabotaged my own wellness. I didn't think that caring for

surely your goodness
and Love will
follow me all the
days of my life,
and I will
dwell in the house
of the Lord forever.
Psalm 23:6

myself was spiritual or that prioritizing my needs was as important—or sometimes even more important—as meeting the needs of others. But in time it was clear I needed a change or my soul center was going to break down. Slowly, I began to make the necessary shifts.

Keeping a Sabbath has grown my trust in the Lord. Good bedtimes and sleep help my body feel so much better and able to work. Hanging out with friends and family I love dearly fills me with joy that also fuels me. Seeing my counselor regularly helps me regulate my emotions and process things happening in my life. Limiting the time I spend on my digital devices brings more clarity to my mind. Limiting the people who have my phone number, as well as the hours when they can reach me, helps to reduce the pressure of demands. I am learning to honor my working hours and close down my computer for the day at 5:00 p.m. more often.

These little tweaks have brought big peaks. I feel more energy and strength as I move through a day. To my surprise, my productivity and the quality of my work both improved. The lie that I had to run harder and produce more in order to be better and more valuable became clear. Such beliefs were actually *limiting* me.

We live in a world that denies God and replaces him with digital devices, with fast-paced, on-the-go schedules, with cheap, nutritionally deficient foods, with shortcuts and hacks and quick fixes. Slowing down to honor God, putting our phones away, looking into each other's eyes, and filling ourselves with things that bring us joy nurture the soul and strengthen it to bear the weight of life.

Your soul is worth tending to. *You're* worth it. You matter, and there is help and hope for you. Life sometimes moves so fast and is so full, you might think, *How in the world would I slow down to even take inventory? Who else would get these things done?* I get it. But finding and tending to the root of your troubles at the soul level is vital for a healthy life. Remember, every fruit has a root. Is your soul rooted in Christ and the fruit of the Spirit? Or is it rooted in the things of the world that yield fruits of chaos, anxiety, exhaustion, and intense pressure?

The soul that is rooted in Christ and grounded in his love can know a strength that surpasses human ability. This alone is what will give us the power to stand strong in the days we are living in, even in life's hardest circumstances.

You may want to implement all of these practices, or perhaps only a few. They have certainly benefited me, and as they become habits, I've begun to experience the true fruit of the Spirit in my life. The restoration journey is not about becoming perfect. It's about becoming our best selves for the purposes of God and the benefit of others. As Parker Palmer said, "Self-care is never a selfish act—it is simply good stewardship of the only gift I have, the gift I was put on earth to offer others. Anytime we can listen to true self and give it the care it requires, we do it not only for ourselves, but for the many others whose lives we touch."[4]

> *The restoration journey is not about becoming perfect. It's about becoming our best selves for the purposes of God and the benefit of others.*

You are *worthy* of caring for yourself.

Part of my prayer for you is reflected in Paul's prayer for the Ephesians:

> For this reason I bow my knees before the Father, from whom every family in heaven and on earth is named, that according to the riches of his glory he may grant you to be strengthened with power through his Spirit in your inner being, so that Christ may dwell in your hearts through faith—that you, being rooted and grounded in love, may have strength to comprehend with all the saints what is the breadth and length and height and depth, and to know the love of Christ that surpasses knowledge, that you may be filled with all the fullness of God.
>
> Now to him who is able to do far more abundantly than all that we ask or think, according to the power at work within us, to him be glory in the church and in Christ Jesus throughout all generations, forever and ever. Amen. (3:14–21)

It's been weeks since I set down my readied sledgehammer.

I watch as the construction crew brings in a huge, beautiful beam, places it high between the kitchen and living room, and secures it. Then the wall comes down and the light flows in.

RESTORATION PRACTICE

Choose Your Hard

Caring for yourself in the day-to-day rhythms of life and following healthy habits of soul care will help support the weight of a life. In the context of soul care, this means pausing to evaluate where your soul-care habits (or lack thereof) are taking you, making course corrections where necessary, and adopting new habits that might feel hard. Does the prospect of doing hard things scare you? Someone once advised me to "choose your hard," and it changed my life.

What is running your life right now? What is at your center? What hard thing are you willing to choose that will make that center stronger? Wise choices take effort and commitment. Start small. Choose one or two things from one of the soul-care lists in this chapter and put them into practice this week. If it helps, keep going and change it up for the next week. Change isn't always easy, but living exhausted, burned-out, and lower than your potential is harder.

9

THE PILLARS OF PURPOSE

God's Vision for Your Life Is Good

I'm smiling at my computer, reading an email that somehow feels significant. It's from someone I've never even met. There's a tingle of fresh excitement in me that I haven't felt in a while when reading inquiries from my website for people interested in my photography sessions.

The email is from a woman in Fork River, New Jersey, a little town tucked two hours south of New York City. She's asking if I still do photography for families and says she has "a rather large crew." She goes on to explain she is a mama to ten precious children—nine adopted internationally, one biological. Eight of her kids are deaf, and two have special needs. She says her family is on a "unique heavenly assignment." The Barsch family is in the beginning stages of building a discipleship ministry called "House of Mending" in order to see broken hearts restored. She says the desire to begin this ministry in their home was birthed out of "their own crushing of the enemy against their marriage and family." I read every line of this email like I'm studying it for a test—every bit of it feels like something special to me.

Over the years I've become more hesitant to travel to places and meet people I don't know unless there is some mutual connection, and I don't know anything about this woman. But my heart feels *drawn* to this shoot, like it's more than just my work. Maybe it's a heavenly assignment for me as well.

I click over to my calendar for the dates she's requesting in the email and see I've got another session scheduled around the same time with someone in NYC, and I know this is meant to be. I'll pair the two shoots together in the same trip and make this happen. I send her a reply to let her know I'd be honored to come capture photographs for her precious crew.

Weeks later, I pull up to their home in my rental car and feel a rush of hesitancy as I park in their driveway. *I don't know these people, and here I am in New Jersey about to knock on their door and go in their house? Is this the right thing to do?* I pray and feel blessed assurance settle in my heart. Taking my heavy gear out of the trunk, I pause for a moment at the back of the car, take a deep breath, then walk up the front steps to their door. Suddenly the door swings open and I'm being welcomed by two of the kindest smiles I could imagine—it's Andrew and Michelle Barsch.

"WELCOME, Meshali! We are so glad to have you. Come on in. Can we help you? Can we take your gear for you? Would you like anything to drink or eat?"

I immediately sense the presence of Jesus in their home. They invite me in and surround me with their kindness, humility, and gratitude for my trip to come work with them. As I round the corner, I see a long table—seated around it are ten precious children looking back at me and reflecting love, joy, peace, and glory as best I can imagine on human faces. Andrew and Michelle sign to them as I greet them with my words, hugs, and smiles.

We circle up in the backyard and I begin to take their photographs. One by one, the children step up and smile so beautifully. Each of them reflects the imago Dei. Eyes bright, smiles kind. Some are a bit hesitant, so Andrew, Michelle, and I give them a little extra encouragement. They light up when I show them a preview of their own images on the screen. Then they stand together as a family, and as my camera clicks repeatedly, I see it: true purpose. The Barsch family is living it out. I see kingdom. Family. Home.

There's something uniquely special about finding our true purpose. Especially when the road is marked with tragedy and pain.

Just six months after giving birth to her first child, Katherine Wolf suffered a catastrophic stroke caused by a congenital brain defect she didn't even know she had. After a sixteen-hour brain surgery, forty days in the ICU, a year in neuro rehab, eleven operations, and fifteen years of rehabilitation, she is still in recovery. Today, together with her husband, Jay, she runs Hope Heals Camps and brings joy into the lives of families affected by disability and chronic pain.[1]

As a young man in the 1960s, Phil Robertson struggled with alcoholism and infidelity, and in 2020 he learned he had fathered a daughter from a long-ago affair.[2] But thanks to the power of his relationship with God and the enduring love and forgiveness of his wife, Kay, Phil's family is inspiring people around the world by their example of how families can grow stronger together in love and grace. The Robertsons spread the good news of God's mercy through their staggeringly popular TV show *Duck Dynasty* and the recently released film *The Blind*.

In her book *In Pursuit of Love*, Rebecca Bender tells the story of how she was trafficked into high-end Las Vegas escort services as a young woman and her anything-but-easy journey to get out. Today she helps other trafficked women escape the life and find their purpose through Elevate Academy, the world's largest online school for trafficking survivors.[3]

There is no shortage of stories about people who have mined the struggles, pain, and tragedies of their lives for meaning and value. What do they often find? That the very thing they would have avoided, if only they could have, has granted them strength and purpose. Some of these people have become what I think of as celebrity servants. Others minister quietly, with no fanfare or recognition but a strength of faith that changes the lives of those around them. Sometimes when I think about these people I wonder, *What if they had given up in their pain? What would the world be missing if it wasn't for their choice to lean into the restoration process and rise up?*

We all need to know there's a reason we exist outside of just ourselves. Our regular eight-to-five. Our normal daily routines. A reason for both our joys and our sorrows. We were made for more.

I was graduating from high school when *The Purpose Driven Life* by Pastor Rick Warren was exploding in popularity. Today, more than twenty years after its publication date, it has sold over 35 million copies. I believe this is because we all have a built-in, God-given desire to know our purpose. Why are we here? What are our lives for?

Even Jesus himself came to earth on a mission, for a purpose. His call on earth was to bring salvation to each one of us. "For the Son of Man came to seek and to save the lost" (Luke 19:10). I often think of this and how his purpose propelled him through life and pain. It was purpose that pushed him onward to the cross when he prayed "not my will, but yours, be done" in the garden of Gethsemane (Luke 22:42).

I don't know about you, but if I could choose, I'd vote for a path to my purpose that didn't go through pain and suffering. Can you imagine knowing your purpose would lead to agony and physical death? But Jesus didn't run away. He was focused on eternity, something *much* bigger than his immediate circumstances.

I have spent a lot of time with people who ask, "How can I find my purpose? What do you think my calling is?" I feel we tend to overcomplicate this question. For one, as disciples of Jesus, our mission is extremely clear. Our general purpose as believers boils down quite simply to loving God and loving others, fulfilling the Great Commission in whatever way we are personally equipped to do that (Matt. 28:16–20).

What experiences have you had that equip you with empathy?

What people are on the path with you?

What skills do you possess that you can offer?

There's not a person reading this book who doesn't have both great worth *and* purpose in the sight of God. They were woven into the fabric of who we are from the beginning. The apostle Paul wrote, "[God] chose us in him before the foundation of the world, that we should be holy and blameless before him. In love he predestined us for adoption to himself as sons through Jesus Christ, according to the purpose of his will" (Eph. 1:4–5). So if you are among those who have ever thought your history, your trauma, your pain, your sin, or your brokenness disqualifies you from the purposes of God, I challenge you to turn that belief on its head.

Nothing that has happened to you and *nothing* that you have done could ever ruin God's vision for your life.

Photography is more than a career to me. My love for creativity, arts, people, story, and seeing beyond the surface into something deeper has always been a part of who I am. My family tells me when I was little I was often the kid who would sit in the room with the adults and just listen to their stories. They said I wouldn't talk much, I would just listen. As I got older that morphed, and my love for telling stories through photography emerged.

When I was in college I saved up my money and bought a Canon 35mm film camera and started taking pictures of pretty much anyone who would let me. I just loved capturing photos of people and favored the images that told stories. Something about this made me feel alive and fueled me in a way not much else did at the time. My wiring—that is, how God made me—has also combined with my experiences to produce characteristics in me that have informed my calling. In college, I studied counseling and worked on my master's degree in social work. As my photography career took off, I was just walking more and more into my purpose. My career is changing in the present moment, shifting a bit. I'm doing photography, but I'm also traveling and sharing my heart through speaking, podcasting, writing a book. Bringing beauty into the world has always brought me great joy and fulfillment. At this point in my life, the Lord is merging all of these passions.

Wherever we are, wherever our feet carry us on any given day, we are in ministry to God through service to others.

The ways in which we love God and love others can take on many different forms through the work we do, whether it's in our jobs, our families and friendships, or our ministries. I have always said *every* believer is called into ministry—the ministry of love. This is true whether you are a teacher, a dentist, a lawyer, a store clerk, a parent, a partner, a neighbor. Wherever we are, wherever our feet carry us on any given day, we are in ministry to God through service to others.

On a really practical level, I think often we can find out some details about our purpose and the work that is right for us by answering a few questions about what stirs our spirit to life:

- What makes you come alive? What brings you joy?
- What needs do you see in the world, culture, or human lives that sit heavy on your heart?
- Where do you want to bring help and change?
- What would you do in your life right now even if you weren't paid to do it?

Our purpose is usually found where the answers to these questions intersect.

Too often we attach the concept of purpose to things like influence or success rather than to the image of God in us and his love being expressed through us. What is the thumbprint of God in your life? When people look at you and your work, what will they see of him? This is where we must first consider our purpose in order to find real security in doing what we were meant to do.

Pillars, like foundations and support beams, help to distribute the weight and protect the structural integrity of a building. While load-bearing beams run horizontally, pillars stand vertically. They're rooted in the foundation and help to hold up other critically important elements of the structure. Pillars tend to be more visible than the beams and foundation. They work out in the open, functioning in plain sight, and reflect the overall design of the architecture just as our purpose reflects the design of our lives.

Our purpose reflects our design.

Have you ever seen pillars on a house that didn't match its design? Like fancy Corinthian columns holding up a farmhouse porch roof? Looks a little off to me! I don't harbor any suspicions that God's purpose for me is to be an astronaut or a boxer or a brain surgeon. Other roles make much more sense.

Don't put God in a box of rigid expectations. Fulfilling your purpose could look like many things, but what matters is the substance. As we follow the Lord and fulfill his commands—loving God, loving people, and being faithful to follow his Word—purpose finds us.

I sometimes wonder about the person I would be today if I had a different story. As much as I struggle to reconcile the harder parts of my life and why they happened, I often wonder who I would be if I had not gone through them and walked to the other side with Jesus. I had a choice: live according to the *trauma narrative* or live according to the *kingdom narrative*. The trauma narrative declares my life is ruined beyond hope. The kingdom narrative includes a promise that God will take the brokenness of my life and bring beauty and redemption, not only for me but for others as well.

The divorce of my parents and the abuse I suffered as a kid were some of the hardest and most formative dynamics of my early life. For so long I looked at those events and their aftermath as being only "bad" things. Today I see that when I surrendered that pain to the Lord, I gave him permission to use those very hardships in shaping me into the person needed to fulfill my purpose and call in life.

Now when I look into the eyes of someone who has experienced abuse, I see them through a lens of empathy. I see myself in them when they share with me that they feel hopeless about it and need the Lord's help so desperately. I remember. I have compassion and tenacity to walk with them through it, even when it feels slow. I remember. When someone is walking through a divorce, my heart aches for them and for their children, and I try to minister to them from all angles. I remember. When I see a person who has a loved one dealing with addiction and they feel betrayed and confused and frustrated with it all—I remember.

God wants to bring goodness out of everything in your life and mind— even the pain.

God has taken what the enemy meant for harm and evil in my life and used it to produce good things.

When I was going through some dark times, a few people said to me, "God is going to use you so mightily." I have never loved the verbiage "God wants to use you," but with the grace of hindsight I understand the encouragement they were trying to offer me. In the Redeemer's hands, everything bad is turned around for good. I don't pretend to know exactly how that works—but a great and loving God in his power and sovereignty knows exactly how. What I believe with all my heart is that God wants to bring goodness out of *everything* in your life and mind— even the pain. If we allow it, we can work with God to save lives.

God never wastes pain.

The Greek word for endurance is *hupomoné* (pronounced hoop-om-on-ay), which embodies steadfastness, patience, perseverance, and constancy. In the New Testament, the word was used to describe a person who doesn't swerve from their purpose or their loyalty, even when that resolve includes suffering.

I've always had a special spot in my heart for Joseph, who was sold into slavery by his brothers, falsely accused of rape by Potiphar's wife, and imprisoned for years. If you don't know his story, you can read it in Genesis 37–45. Joseph's suffering began when he was a teenager. He was a victim of jealous, greedy, powerful people—starting with his own brothers—who used him to accomplish their own evil intentions.

Joseph was a dreamer, and dreaming was what got Joseph into trouble in the first place. He might have talked a little too freely about dreams he had of becoming a great man. Anyone who had known about those dreams might have mocked him during his years in an Egyptian prison. "Who do you think you are?" they might have said. "Who do I think I am?" he might have agreed. When someone in the prison needed a dream interpreted, Joseph might have stayed silent and thought, *Dreaming gets me into trouble. I don't do that anymore. I want nothing to do with your dreams.* Instead, he gave the man a good interpretation. And years later, when Pharaoh himself needed a dream interpreted, someone remembered Joseph's skill and brought Joseph out of the prison at just the right time to save the whole nation of Egypt from a famine, as well as the family who had sold him away.

"God sent me before you to preserve for you a remnant on earth, and to keep alive for you many survivors," Joseph said to his shocked brothers, who feared his revenge. "So it was not you who sent me here, but God" (Gen. 45:7–8). Later, when they asked for his forgiveness, he repeated, "You meant evil against me, but God meant it for good, to bring it about that many people should be kept alive, as they are today" (Gen. 50:20).

God did not cause Joseph's suffering; his family did. But God did not allow Joseph's experiences to go to waste. Only God can somehow use even the worst parts of our story and bring beauty and redemption. This is restoration.

God's Word says that suffering is sometimes the catalyst for the production of fruit in our lives. The apostle Paul writes, "Not only that, but we rejoice in our sufferings, knowing that suffering produces endurance, and endurance produces character, and character produces hope, and hope does not put us to shame, because God's love has been poured into our hearts through the Holy Spirit who has been given to us" (Rom. 5:3–5). This Scripture gives me deep hope in hard times, especially when those hard times seem *long*.

> *Only God can somehow use even the worst parts of our story and bring beauty and redemption.*

Joseph was separated from his family for more than two decades, and he spent thirteen of those years enslaved and unjustly imprisoned. But in that Romans passage, Paul is saying there is purpose in our pain beyond what we can see or feel right now, and God is creating something in us through that. This is why we have to let hard seasons play out and do their work in us. We want to sometimes pray suffering away and escape it prematurely. We want relief more than we want wisdom. But some of the hardest times in my life have actually produced the greatest fruits in the end.

And I am still walking through some of these times. Waiting has been a big theme of my life. There's a reason why patience is sometimes called "long-suffering." While I wouldn't wish some of my experiences on anyone, I do know that God has been building endurance in my spirit over the years. It's easy to trust God when I have everything that I want so badly. But what about when I don't have those things? Do I have endurance to wait for them to come? Can I trust him if he says what I want wouldn't be good for me? Can I trust that he's good even when my hands are empty of some things my heart desires?

I think of how Joseph named one of his sons Ephraim, which means "God has made me fruitful in the land of my suffering" (Gen. 41:52 NIV). Following God through all of life's hardships produced fruitfulness not only for Joseph but for his posterity. God always has more than just you or me in mind. He is thinking of others, of our fruitfulness. God himself fills the void that suffering opens in us. Through this we come to truly know him, and then through us others come to know him in a new and powerful way.

The shoot is over, and Andrew comes up next to me.

"Meshali, is it okay if we pray for you?"

I've been so touched by them all afternoon that this makes me want to cry tears of joy. I reply with a quick "YES, absolutely!"

They surround me with words of encouragement, blessing, and love in their prayer.

As I go to leave, Michelle hands me a bag and tells me they all made this gift bag last night and to open it at the airport. Andrew says, "We prayed for you as a family last night as well, and we did an exercise with our kids while they sat at the table, asking them to write out their exact prayer for you and draw a picture of what they saw."

There is no chance I can wait until I get to the airport to open this bag.

I thank them profusely and bid them goodbye before climbing back into my rental.

Partway to the airport, I stop and look inside the bag. One by one, I open up ten precious handwritten notes. The pictures the kids drew for me are so bright and vivid, with precious words underneath. They

speak of what these kids saw in me when they prayed for me before even meeting me yet—all of which is a reminder to me of my purpose.

> *When I pray for you, I see you teaching lots of people about the Bible. I see Jesus giving a lot of people communion too. I think you look like Jesus. I'm happy you decided to come take pictures of my family. I think it's going to be a beautiful day. Love, Elliana, age 8*

> *Dear Meshali, I am glad you have Holy Spirit in your heart. I think it's so cool that you are a photographer. Thank you so much for coming to our family! I pray you can tell everyone in Texas about Jesus. Thank you again! Love, Paloma, age 13*

> *I'm praying you will teach lots of people about having Jesus in their hearts. I think I can be friends with you. I have Down syndrome and I lived in Texas before I was adopted. I love my family and pictures and I love that you love Jesus. I love ice cream too. Love, Julie*

I can hardly keep it together. Tears stream down my face as I carefully handle each precious piece of paper, souvenirs I know I'll keep forever.

On any given day, if I look for it, I can find any and every reason in the world why someone else is a better fit for this work that's been put before me. I can always find someone more equipped, more educated, more eloquent, more gritty, more up to the task. Plenty of photographers in the world are more famous, more experienced, or more skilled than I am. When I find myself feeling this way, I know I need a change in perspective—a shift in what I'm looking *at* or looking *for* or looking *to*. When my eyes are on myself as the source and reasoning for my purpose, I lose strength and I lose traction. But when I keep my focus on *God*, the one who is the reason behind my purpose and who is able to sustain me in my purpose, I gain strength.

Now, the healthier I feel and am, the more fueled I am for purpose. When I'm tending to those load-bearing soul-care habits—growing in faith, nourishing my body, resting, exercising, partaking in great community, seeing my counselor regularly—those things accumulate and make it easier to fulfill my purpose.

But I'm grateful the pressure is not on me. The only responsibilities I have in fulfilling my purpose are to be obedient to God's call and to trust the All-Powerful One who is able to make the rest happen—and this often means getting out of my own way. This means I have to stop thinking my weakness is greater than God's strength. I have to stop thinking that everything relies on my own power, my own worthiness, or my own ability.

Peace comes when we know we don't have to be perfect to fulfill our purpose, because we serve the one who *is* perfect and able and who will give us the power to achieve whatever he asks of us.

RESTORATION PRACTICE

Remember

Take as much time as you need to reflect on your history. Acknowledge the bad—the suffering, the pain. Then look for experiences in your life that followed and how they reveal the fruits of endurance, character, and hope that God is producing in you (Rom. 5:3–5). What beauty, strength, and purpose have emerged or are emerging from these experiences?

10

THE
BUTTRESS
OF
COMMUNITY

You Don't Have to Do It Alone

I'm drowning in a lake of my own tears.

I'm curled up on my bed in my silent, cold farmhouse, where I can hear the sound of my own lament bouncing off the bare walls and floors. This pain in my gut, this battle I'm fighting by myself, has reduced me to a place that I know won't sustain me any longer.

I'm about to do something that scares me.

I lift my head off my wet pillow, pushing back the strands of hair that stick to my face and tucking them behind my ears. I pick up my phone and dial the number that's on my heart.

"Hello?"

My unstable dam breaks again as I weep at the sound of my friend Leah's voice and warble through my own greeting.

"Meshali, what's wrong? Are you okay?"

My moment of truth has arrived. "I'm not okay," I confess. And then I make a bold move. "Can you make a trip here? I just feel I need someone here with me right now. I need to talk this out and talk in person."

I've never asked anyone for anything like this before. I've never been this vulnerable or expressed my own needs like this before, not even with a friend. My precious friend Leah lives in Nashville; she's a woman with so much on her plate. She leads a busy life as a pastor, wife, and mother of two amazing boys. Her life is full of commitments and events.

"Yes."

Within twenty-four hours she's on a flight.

When I think back on that devastating day now, my memory doesn't focus on the heartache and brokenness I felt. Instead, I recall an unexpected gift of love and grace. My history after trauma has made it difficult to trust people. And this particular heartache came after a broken relationship brought me to my knees. I need and want close relationships, but at the time I was battling with the push and pull of allowing people close, then being frightened by intimacy. Some unhealthy interpersonal patterns had crept back into my life, poisoning my thinking and making my struggles more intense. When this struggle cycled through yet another crushing round of pain and tears, I recognized that I was attempting to fight my battles alone. I knew I needed more healing and transformation in my heart. I knew God wanted me to invite someone in.

My sweet friend Leah flew to see me, sat at my farmhouse with me, listened to me, talked with me, processed with me, and spoke *life* into my very difficult situation. I immediately started to feel better, and a big wave of healing came to my life soon after this, making it easier for me to trust the strength of true friends willing to walk with me through hard things.

I began to experience new freedom—the freedom that comes from not being alone.

Foundations support a home from below. Load-bearing beams support from above. Pillars support from within. And buttresses support from outside. They're designed to protect against forces that would make a wall buckle, bulge, crack, or fall over. Like foundations, beams, and pillars, buttresses help to redistribute weight so that a wall can bear more. In any person's life, a healthy community of loved ones offers a reliable, dependable, solid, helpful buttress against the winds of life.

Who wouldn't want that?

I didn't, at first.

I would have *told* you I wanted it, but something was in the way of my reaching out for it. What stopped me from inviting others into the sacred spaces of my pain for so long? It wasn't for lack of opportunity. I love being around people, hearing their stories, extending encouragement and compassion. But I've attended more than one dinner where I couldn't keep the focus from eventually coming around to me. I recall one night in particular when the tables turned and someone asked me a question about my story, and I became the center of attention.

I felt the blood drain from my face and the drop of my stomach as panic and insecurity settled over me like someone threw a weighted blanket on my body. Disconnected pieces of my story flashed before my eyes like cards on a storyboard, nothing in place. Where would I even begin? *How* could I begin?

I answered the question in a very high-level, surface-skimming way, mentioning where I grew up, what I had done in college, and how my professional career got its start. I realized how hard it was for me to be vulnerable with any meaningful details.

Now, I don't believe in spilling your guts to every single person who asks about your story—but this conversation didn't happen at a dinner table with casual acquaintances. It happened at a table with people who I considered to be great friends. Despite my caring, empathetic heart for those people and *their* stories, my self-protective fear of failure and inadequacy was alive and well that day.

I didn't know it at the time, but risk was standing in my way of building a meaningful community.

Risk of being rejected.

Risk of being misunderstood.

Risk of being abandoned.

Risk of others' poor opinions of me.

Risk of losing the people I cared about the most.

Underneath all this risk is an old emotion that we try to manage or suppress because it tells us we are unworthy of community, unworthy of being loved, and maybe even unworthy of this life.

That emotion is shame.

Shame attempts to isolate us, cut us off, shut us down. With a history of brokenness, we learn to hide. We hide from the pain of addictions, abuse, abandonment, illness, dysfunction, divorce. These things have a way of locking us up, but in that prison we think we are safe. Circumstances put me in that prison, but I was the one who locked the door, sealed it up tight, and threw away the key.

Trauma had trained me to be quiet. To pretend things were okay when they weren't. There was a point in my life where I had carried the pain trauma handed to me and had kept quiet for so long and felt so devastated on the inside that I really wasn't sure I could continue on. I never wanted to take my life, but I came to a place where my will to live and my zest for life just weren't there anymore. I was hopeless, isolated, and so tired from the inner fight.

Today, when I look at that memory from the outside, I have compassion for that Meshali. Things had happened to me that I didn't understand. I had done things as a result of my brokenness, and I was unable to make sense of any of it. I tried to deal with it alone, with nothing more than my own thoughts, my own processes, my own energy and strength, and I felt overwhelmed. A constant internal bully kept telling me, "Something is wrong with you." That voice is hard to fight when you feel alone.

And the remedy for that might be the very thing we fear most: raw vulnerability with trustworthy people.

"Shame dies when stories are told in safe places," writes author Ann Voskamp.[1] And counselor Ed Welch says, "[God] hears and knows what is in your heart, which is where you fret, hide, love, hate, desire, and feel. When someone knows what is in your heart and that person loves you all the more rather than turns away from you, you are more inclined to stop hiding and start talking."[2]

A safe place—where at least one loving and trustworthy person stands with you through thick and thin—is all a person needs to have an experience of being in meaningful relationship. A community is a similar experience on a slightly larger scale. It includes more than one person, and ideally three types of people:

1. *People who pour into you.* These are mentors and role models who are further down the road than you in certain areas of life. These are friends who offer you insight, encouragement, wisdom, and hope. They don't race off and leave you alone in the dust, but have the extraordinary gift of patience; they make time for you when you need them. They might even hop on a plane from another city to pay you a visit when you're in crisis.

2. *People who are your peers.* These are fellow travelers who can empathize with you because they are experiencing or have experienced similar struggles and heartaches. Though they might still be in the midst of suffering, they're also present to the truth that the journey is a little easier if it isn't undertaken alone. These are the people who know that sitting beside each other in silent compassion is sometimes all you need—or all you can take. But they also know from experience when it's time to say just the right word.

3. *People* you *pour into.* A healthy community is a place where you can give as well as receive. In community your purpose and service are welcome, and sometimes that service will involve opportunities to give others the same kind of comfort and support you have needed (2 Cor. 1:4; 1 Pet. 4:10).

This helpful model of "people before you, people beside you, people behind you" can help you identify the overall health of the community you're in—and where you might be experiencing gaps.

Community is vital to our well-being, to really living at our fullest. We need perspectives, experiences, and voices that are outside of ourselves—and sometimes that are truly beyond us—to get the breadth of encouragement, support, and strength we need. Only in community can we have that life-giving experience of feeling seen, known, and loved even in our rawest form.

I know that the topic of community is tender for some. You might have experienced your greatest wounding in community. Or maybe you have longed for community seemingly forever, only to feel disappointed time and time again. I think of how Jesus took his friends with him to Gethsemane to keep watch and pray with him while he faced his most desperate, darkest hour . . . and they fell asleep (Matt. 26:36–46). Later, they ran away and denied knowing him at all.

A healthy community is a place where you can give as well as receive.

Jesus knows what you're experiencing.

Good community isn't easy to find and maintain. Many difficulties can stand in the way of meeting people with whom we have authentic connections. Can you trust God to bring these people into your life—and you into theirs—at just the right time? Maybe some of these tips that have helped me can help you too:

- Pray that Jesus would bring healthy community into your life. God-appointed friendships are the best.
- Plant yourself in a healthy church community and keep your heart open and on the lookout for friends.
- Make the first move to be a friend to others. Sometimes we have to be the ones to initiate the relationship, even when it's uncomfortable or inconvenient.
- Step outside your comfort zone.
- Be verbal with others about your need for community and solid friendships. Ask for what you want!
- Look for what others need and ways you can help. Sometimes your "pillar of purpose" is a wide-open door into community.
- Confess to God your judgments, prejudices, or other attitudes that keep you isolated from others. Ask him to help you get out of your own way.

I sit in Peggy's office and talk to her for the first time, opening up to her about my story. The wall I've built around my heart feels like it's starting to crumble at this plain wooden table in this church. Something about Peggy and the way she's talking to me makes me feel . . . free. Free to talk and be myself, and free to be loved fully.

I wipe my tears from my face as I finish and open my eyes to see Peggy lovingly staring at me.

"I'm so sorry you have walked through any of this feeling alone," she says gently to me. "I am so honored you shared it with me. You are so loved, Meshali, and so very valuable. I am so proud of you for sharing this part of your heart and journey. I know that took great courage."

She doesn't break eye contact with me as she continues.

"You are brave," she says. "You are courageous. You are loved. Jesus has such compassion for you, Meshali. Jesus has seen it all and wants to help you. Jesus loves you in your weakness. He doesn't need you to be strong—he is. You can rest."

That was the exact day my shame started to die.

We were made to be known, to love and be deeply loved. I would have to allow God to rewire my brain to believe this. I would have to relearn being loved. But that was the day I took the first step to healing and wholeness, body, mind, and soul.

Killing the voice of shame is never instant but is a process. The day I dealt shame the death blow was the day I chose vulnerability and started to let others in, beginning with Peggy. It took a couple years of restoration work before I extended this to close friends like Leah, but meeting with Peggy had been my huge first step.

Peggy gave me a true gift in her words that day. I think about her reaction to my vulnerability as a blueprint of how to respond to people when they open up to me about something hard. With love, kindness, truth . . . and a big side of compassion. My experience was a catalyst to my being able to open up to others in my life—and to invite them to open up with me—in real, raw ways.

Once I made the firm decision to stop living in isolation, I drew boundaries. I didn't pour my heart out to people in the same way I spoke candidly and without reservation in the security of my counselor's presence. Learning to be appropriate with what we share is part of being healthy. But as I began to slowly open up and build that love and trust with God and others, I felt more and more free. This was a game-changing step forward for me. When discerning what to share with a trusted friend or member of a community, here's what I've found helpful in my own life: I figure out which essential details my friend needs for understanding the situation, the primary feeling I'm struggling to work through, and perhaps a related question I want them to help me think through.

I've always been more private by nature, and I've learned that's okay. But I've also learned it's not good for our souls to live in isolation. About two years ago, I learned the term *ambivert*. An ambivert, they say, is a person who identifies as both an extrovert (a person who is energized and refueled by being with people) and an introvert (a person who is energized and refueled by solitude). Historically I've identified as an introvert, but on my journey toward restoration I have come to recognize that my time with people can also be profoundly energizing. I need people as much as I need my time alone. Regardless of which "-vert" best describes you, there's a principle here that has nothing to do with personality. Even the world's most self-proclaimed loners are wired for relationship, friendship, and companionship. Ideally, we allow ourselves to be known and loved by God first, and then, safe in his love, we can find our footing in true community with others.

> *Our restoration doesn't take place in a vacuum. Healing requires something of us vertically with God and horizontally with others.*

We have a part to play in this community-building endeavor. Our restoration doesn't take place in a vacuum. Healing requires something of us vertically with God and horizontally with others. James 5:16 instructs us in this: "Confess your faults *one to another* [horizontal], and *pray one for another* [vertical], that ye may be *healed*" (KJV). It's in the confession to one another that we find healing and are able to receive prayer.

I knew the vulnerability I had first experienced with Peggy needed to be an ongoing practice for me. The Lord began to sovereignly place people in my life. For a few years I worked as a recruiter at a university while finishing my undergrad degree and then starting graduate school. A counseling professor a couple doors down from me befriended me and stopped by my office periodically to chat. One day she asked, "Would you like to meet once a week for lunch and chat?" From that day on, she became a dear friend. I began to attend the church where she and her husband pastor, and became grounded in community and meaningful friendships. All of this began to transform me, slowly but surely. Even on days when I didn't "feel" connected, the relationships with healthy people were changing me, encouraging me, challenging me, holding me accountable, cheering me on. I was doing something similar for others. All of it was doing a healing work inside of me.

Finding and choosing which people to let into your inner circle and most tender heart space should be bathed in prayer and wisdom. Healthy community plays a part in your healing, and unhealthy community will play a part in your remaining broken and stuck. I can't stress enough how important it is to choose your community wisely. I don't mean looking for perfect individuals—there is no community made up of perfect people. But avoid those spaces where people are more concerned with gossip, manipulation, power grabs, judgment, and exclusion. Ask a counselor to help you identify blind spots where you might be conditioned to trust untrustworthy people. (Counseling is a great place to begin breaking old life patterns that no longer serve you.) When I'm looking for healthy community, I look for people who are kind, loyal, humble, caring, compassionate, wise, and sincere listeners. You'll have your own list. Don't be afraid to hold people to a certain standard. When the Bible tells us to guard our heart (Prov. 4:23), it's talking about guarding the "wellsprings of life" in us. Don't let those waters be poisoned.

> *Healthy community plays a part in your healing, and unhealthy community will play a part in your remaining broken and stuck.*

On the day I poured my heart out to Peggy, nothing yet had changed externally other than I felt more known and loved. A spotlight shined on my soul. I was seen. I had been found out. And I was loved anyway. And that began to change me.

Feeling loved in the deepest places spurred me to know that not only was it okay to be vulnerable with trusted voices, but it was necessary for my healing. I didn't need someone to love a version of me I projected. I didn't have the strength to keep up the illusion! I needed to be loved for the real me by someone who was aware of my pain and brokenness and neediness, my inability to produce or perform. I set down any pride that would keep me isolated. I couldn't fight the voices in my head alone anymore in my own strength. I needed to follow Jesus's model of community, inviting others into my pain and having them join me in the fight for restoration.

Today I want to speak to you what Peggy spoke to me:

Jesus has compassion for you.

Jesus has seen it all and wants to help you.

Jesus loves you in your weakness.

He doesn't need you to be strong—he is.

You can rest.

This is true right now, right where you are, with no prerequisite of already starting your restoration journey. I am not speaking to a future version of you but to the person you are today, with all the strengths and weaknesses you bring to the table.

You are chosen and deeply loved by God.

RESTORATION PRACTICE

Reach Out to Someone Behind You

Think about a person you have noticed who might need an invitation into community. Maybe you don't know this person well, but you've seen them standing on the margins of life. How can you let them know you have seen them? What could you do to come alongside them as a fellow traveler and express the love of Jesus to them?

11

WAITING IN THE MESS

You Are Loved Unconditionally

Friends and family have spent the afternoon congratulating me. Just about everyone who has walked alongside me and cheered me on in the purchase of this fixer-upper dropped in today to celebrate my official move into the house. They bring food and housewarming gifts and help me to move a few essential items of furniture into my new home: my mattress, a flimsy little desk and lamp. All my excitement, anticipation, nervousness, vision, has become a reality.

And now as I wave goodbye to all these dear friends who have homes of their own to return to, I have a chance to rest in the fullness of the reality that the house in all its messy glory really is mine. It's charming and full of character, but beneath the half-empty pizza boxes of our celebration there is my table, resting on old flooring that possibly needs replacement. I gaze into my kitchen that still needs appliances and so many other things. Beside it, in the hall where my laundry is, the walls are uneven and the plumbing needs to be completely ripped out.

All mine.

I turn the doorknob and walk inside. I close the door and am startled by the sudden silence. Has it always been so quiet? The smells of "old home" hit me. I look around, and the weight of reality falls on me like a ton of bricks. Was I wearing blinders when I bought this place? It's charming and full of character, but there is so much work to be done.

When I walked the house with Meredith, all I could see was potential. Now, all I see is the work.

My excitement is still there (hiding now behind a little wall of fear), but also a real sense of responsibility. No one else is going to do this for me.

Maybe I should make a to-do list? No, that would be pointless—there's not enough paper in this house to write out a list like that. I'll take a bath instead. I head toward the only bathroom.

I'm a nightly bath taker. I absolutely *love* a bath, and I go *all out*. I'm talking salts, candles, a playlist, the whole nine yards. Mine is an all-out spa experience. A good, hot bath just makes everything better in my book.

The bathroom has already been gutted, and I put down a new floor before moving in. The cast-iron tub is clean, and the lower half of the walls have been painted, but the upper half of the walls are an unfinished mess, and everything is bare. I realize there are no window coverings in here. I look into the glossy black windowpane and realize I can't see out, but anyone out there could see in. I quickly hang a blanket. What am I going to do about the bedroom? I realize I'm not even sure if the tap works.

I turn the rusty faucets. They squeak and groan, but the water comes out clean and soon hot water fills the tub. I cheer and put the stopper in the drain with great relief. In a few more minutes I'm sinking beneath bubbles and scents that usually calm me. Tonight, though, I'm soaking in a soup of doubt. *Can I really do this?*

My decision to restore the old Carter family home set a miracle in motion in my life, though on that first night, it sure didn't feel like it. A miracle is happening in your life too, even if you can't quite see it.

Jesus is making all things new, but some days it feels like the work—whether restoration of a physical house or the house of our lives—is nothing but a mess. And why is it taking so *long*? Why can't Jesus just wave his miracle-maker hands and help us get this work done faster? Why does he sometimes heal with spit and mud and then require us to go wash ourselves up, rather than sending us to a figurative, sanitized hospital room where trained caregivers wait on our every need (see John 9:6–7)?

Recently, I was thinking about my love of and fascination with before-and-after pictures and before-and-after stories. It's a common thread woven throughout my loves: photography, home restoration, people's stories, my soul. You've seen the before-and-after pictures in this book. Some days I can barely remember the "before" that was this home. When I see those original photos now, I hardly recognize the place—and I surely can't believe I took it on from where it had once been. The feeling that comes looking back on such a transformation is hard to describe.

Is it possible to stand on the "before" side of the mess and have an equally thrilling feeling? I think it is. I call it "seeing beyond"—looking past the evidence of chaos and impossibility to what *might* be.

When we can see past the Insta-perfection of our curated, tidy, picture-perfect lives into the truth, then we can experience hope and healing.

As a photographer, I have to "see beyond" each time I walk into a photo shoot. I have to see beyond the imperfections of a setting and look for the beauty, the negative spaces, the beams of light that break through. I have to see beyond a person's surface appearance and look into their soul, their story, their journey. If I don't, I won't know what I want my camera to capture. I won't be looking at the true person. I talk to them and pull out what makes them smile and laugh, what brings them joy, what moves them. This is the only way I know to capture the real beauty of each person I meet—by seeing past the surface and into what is less obvious but more important. This is how the Holy Spirit sees you and me.

Seeing through Christ's eyes into the beyond is a beautiful way of living, and the Spirit helps us make this possible, whether we are looking into the discouraging spaces of our own messy lives or the brokenness of someone else's. When we can see past the Insta-perfection of our curated, tidy, picture-perfect lives into the truth, then we can experience hope and healing. Then we can invite other people into this shared space where we really see each other and serve each other.

Recently I sat in a waiting room and looked around. Eight people sat alongside me. Every single person was looking down at their phones. I thought about it and wondered: How many were working? How many were doomscrolling? How many were on social media looking at the lives of people they didn't even know? In his book *The Total Money Makeover*, Dave Ramsey says, "We buy things we don't need with money we don't have in order to impress people we don't like."[1] How many people were shopping, spending money they didn't have to impress people they didn't even like? I thought about the grip that phones and social media have on people in our world today. It's not all bad all the time, but it's full of invitations to compare our lives to others. With the touch of a fingertip we can fall into highlight reels, images, vacations, homes, states of being that all look like so much more than we can attain.

If I sat and compared my little 1,446-square-foot farmhouse to the apparently pristine mansions I see from social media influencers, I would never post pictures of my house again.

And I'd be sad if the pictures I post of my home made anyone feel brought low rather than lifted up, which is my intention. Believe me, I spend my days "in the mess." Yes, I make the time to look for beauty, to make beauty, and to capture beauty in images—but my life is as messy as anyone else's.

Sometimes shame keeps us from letting others into our lives until we seemingly have it together. The curated stories of others' lives as presented on social media make us feel as if everyone but us has it together. What does it mean to invite people into our lives while we're in-process?

As I mentioned when talking about the buttress of community, we experience a unique kind of healing when we're vulnerable enough to be known by others. This vulnerability is impossible if we stay in a frame of mind that tempts us to compare the work God is doing in our lives with what he might be doing in the lives of others. We have to stop comparing our insides to other people's outsides, Anne Lamott says.[2] If we don't stop, we will stay stuck in our pain.

How much time do you spend comparing your life to someone else's? We have to fight the temptation to compare ourselves to others, then set up healthy barriers against this way of thinking. Here are a few helpful tips that worked for me in retraining my own mind and heart while waiting on God, written as exercises in encouragement for you.

1. Write down five things you are grateful for that are specific to today.
2. Think about God's attributes—he is good, merciful, loving, beautiful, just, patient (just for starters)—and pick one to focus on today. Decide to look for evidence of it.
3. Name one of your strengths and ask God how he would have you use your strength today.
4. Look beyond your needs to the needs of others. Look for an opportunity to help someone today who needs what you can offer.
5. Compete with yourself, not others. What's one thing you can do today to be a better version of your true, authentic self?

Inviting people into the messy spaces of my home and heart has been a *real* challenge for me. One of the decisions I made when I bought the farmhouse was to do the restoration as I could afford it. I decided to pay cash as I was able to rather than take out a big loan. On the upside, I'm avoiding large debts. On the downside, the restoration takes longer— much longer than I would like. I'm going at my own pace, slow and methodical. At any given moment, I have an incomplete project going on in the house.

We don't have to be fully restored before we can begin welcoming others into the "beyond" beauty of our lives.

I know this, but my perfectionist self *still* shows up when anyone knocks on my door. I feel the need to tidy up. I want to welcome my guest but also explain why things are messy. I put shoes away. I fold blankets and stack books while talking to them. I make a point of talking about whatever project has debris scattered across the floor. And that's just the literal mess of my day-to-day living space. I won't even get into the figurative messiness that you can't see at a glance.

But here's what I've been learning: We might admire the latest home-improvement trend or Pinterest interior decor collection, but deep down people prefer a lived-in home. They feel more comfortable, more able to let their hair down and come in to stay awhile, when things aren't perfectly tidy—whether in the environment or in the hearts of those gathered. They can breathe a little easier and put their feet up. When I remember this, when I take a deep breath and open the door and welcome them in, never mind the dirty cups on the coffee table or the plastic sheeting hanging from the ceiling, I find myself looking at the right thing: the person standing right in front of me. When I set aside my worry about how anyone perceives me, I see them more clearly. I see beyond my circumstances and also beyond theirs.

This is where Jesus meets us.

Last fall I returned from a trip to Nashville, an absolute beauty in that season. I don't know of another person who has such a rich affection for a Tennessee fall day as me. I had visualized that week and planned it out perfectly in my head. My intention was to go to Nashville, spend time soaking in the beauty, see sweet friends, and work on my book during all the glory of autumn. The words I had on my heart for this book—for you—were just going to flow out of me like a river. I would do a couple of shoots and mix work with play. I'd stay with great friends in their beautiful home in the most perfect Tennessee mountain setting. And I did all that.

We work and we wait. We live in the mess, looking forward to the day of restoration and renewal.

But one night as I was laughing among friends—people who know me deeply and love me, and I them—a bit of sadness crept into my heart. It felt like loneliness. I couldn't put my finger on it. I excused myself after dinner, made my way downstairs, got ready for bed, and pulled back the covers. Sliding into them,

I laid my head on the pillow and felt a familiar wave of impatience and questions come over me. The nagging feeling persisted, threatening to weigh me down emotionally. *How in the world am I expected to write this book feeling this way?*

I dozed off, praying and giving my questions to God, applying the practice of casting my cares upon Jesus. As I shifted back and forth, so many exciting things swirled in my mind from all I felt like God was doing in my heart, but paralleled with feelings of doubt and "what-ifs." I thought about how in ways I was still living in the tension of the now and not yet—not just in my home but in each phase of my life. Areas of celebration and areas of want will always coexist. We work and we wait. We live in the mess, looking forward to the day of restoration and renewal. Remember that waiting room, where everyone was looking at their phones? We can wait in eager expectation, taking in the fullness of our surroundings (however mundane they might be), or we can wait and distract ourselves with mind-numbing practices.

Life is sweet and full, but even while many great things are happening for me professionally—even surrounded by great friends and close family—I'm asking the Lord for a few specific desires. I don't know about you, but there are still prayers in my heart that I am believing God will answer but I have not seen come to pass yet. Over and over I take these desires to him and leave them at his feet. As I abide in him and delight myself in him, he puts the desires of my heart in place—and not because God is a vending machine who makes all my orders come to be. But because I've adopted a heart posture of binding myself to him, my heart is being transformed in that my desires become *God's* desires for me.

I'm not married yet, but I would like to be. I have no children, but I hope to. The good news is Jesus knows and he deeply cares. He wants me to come to him with every part of my heart, every desire and longing. I've made it a point to try not to hyperfocus on these things, but they are, quite simply, desires of my heart.

Restoring my farmhouse home in a season of singleness has made the process interesting in ways. I'm restoring the home while working to pay the bills *and* pay for the restoration projects. Sometimes this reality fuels angst. I call these my "If only" days. If only I was in a different life stage . . . If only I had more money . . . If only I was married by now, this would just be easier. We would have two incomes. I would have a live-in shoulder to lean on. We could do the work together.

Some days I sit in my home feeling full of faith and expectation that these things will happen at the right time. Other days I feel scared and hopeless. At times such as those, I have to sit in this tension of waiting, of holding beauty and burden in the same hand. Things feel a bit harder. They feel undone. Sometimes I'm not even sure what I'm waiting for.

You might be amazed how often people exclaim, "You're not married?! Why? How? Do you want to be? Do you want kids?" People's questions can be exhausting sometimes, don't you think? Yes, I want those things. But how am I to know why or how they haven't happened? These questions hit me, and if I'm not careful, I fall into fear: *Did I miss it? Is it too late?* I can only lean into God's mercy and trust him. Right this second, I don't have the answers I want. So I wait. I abide.

I do believe God sometimes allows situations in our lives where the only answer and remedy to our pain is him. This is where he is faithful. This is where he sustains. This is where he brings hope to our hopelessness and shows his power in our weakness. We could choose to lean on idols that can ease the pain, but idols can't bring you the answer you need. Your idol can't heal you. Jesus can and will.

In such moments, in these gaps where my need feels greater than what I hold in my hands, the Lord continues to show himself faithful. If I had a dollar for every time he's shown up for me in the home restoration process, I would be a rich woman. He shows up in all ways, big and small.

My testimony list is a mile long. One example is the time several major repairs were needed all at once. In the span of four weeks, I needed a new roof, the sewer system had cracked and was leaking under the guest bedroom, and the back door was rotting out and needed to be completely replaced. Such issues are not unique to me as the owner of an old house. I know all homeowners face problems like these, and when they all happen at once for us, it's so disheartening.

I cried out to God. "God, I know you see me. I know you are my Father, and I know you care. I commit these needs to you. I believe you are meeting my needs." In times of need or doubt, it is crucial that we cling to truth and not our feelings. In this tension, the enemy will tempt us to think God has forgotten about us or doesn't care about us.

Slowly but surely over those weeks, the Lord met my needs one by one in miraculous ways—and not in ways I expected. My job is to look up and look around me and watch for the ways he's coming through. Heaven is hanging over the banister cheering us on, but we can miss it so easily when our eyes are on our circumstances.

We've talked a lot about the process of restoration—God's process of transforming us, sanctifying us. This is a lifelong process, for you and for me. And so many parts of this process involve waiting. Not one of us has "arrived" everywhere we're meant to be, but we are being transformed in the process.

> *Heaven is hanging over the banister cheering us on, but we can miss it so easily when our eyes are on our circumstances.*

We are all waiting for something. Waiting can be downright hard. There's no getting around it, and none of us escapes the waiting room. We wait for that relationship, for children, for that perfect dream job, for financial breakthrough, for physical and emotional healing. We wait, we hope, we desire, and the ache is real. And we are all being transformed by our obedience to God and our trust in his faithfulness and promises to us—day by day by day.

In the waiting seasons, I have felt both close to God and far away from him. At times I've felt curious, I've felt angry, I've felt resentful, I've felt forgotten. I've also known deep down that I have to wrestle with these feelings. When I do, I think once again of Martha, who never questioned Jesus's ability to heal her brother, Lazarus. But she sure did question his timing. *Where were you? Why did you take so long? See what happened while you stayed away?*

Even in the moments before Jesus raised Lazarus from the dead, he was drawing Martha's attention to a bigger truth. *Yes, I know you wanted me to stop your brother from dying*, Jesus seems to be saying. *But are you ready for something more?* I'm not sure she understood his intentions until her brother walked out of that tomb.

I've heard it said that the lushest growth happens in valleys, not on mountaintops. Have you ever met someone who has overcome a lot in life and is still walking with Christ? There is glory on them, usually a wisdom, an anointing. It's hard to put a finger on, but I have met many people who walk with this special touch from Jesus. Maybe Martha did too. There is something that takes place in our lives, a growth and transformation that I am convinced only comes through facing trials, enduring . . . overcoming. When I allow them to, my questions lead me to Jesus and push me to his feet.

That's where I've always eventually found peace.

I have a dear friend in New York City, Lynette Lewis, who has inspired me greatly over the years as a mentor and encourager. She is a beautiful, thriving, full-of-life, successful woman in her sixties. She married at forty-two, and her words hold a lot of weight with me because of the journey she has walked.

I sent Lynette a voice memo one night when I was a little discouraged, and she told me about a time after her fortieth birthday when her heart was in pain on the road of waiting for marriage. The pain of waiting ebbed and flowed, and sometimes felt unbearable.

One day she wondered how much longer she could handle this "hope deferred" (Prov. 13:12). She was truly heartsick. She sat at a restaurant in NYC eating breakfast with her best friend, who listened to her as she said, "I just don't feel I can wait anymore." The women both had thriving lives that looked very different. Lynette's dear friend was a married woman with ten children, Lynette was unmarried with no kids, but they had walked alongside each other through decades, each supporting the other in her calling.

Her friend, full of empathy, peered across the small table and lovingly said, "I know this is hard, Lynette. We will continue to walk through this together. Can you wait two more weeks?" The question kind of took her aback.

Lynette processed the question and looked back across the table at her and replied, "Yes, I can wait two more weeks."

"Okay," her friend said. "We'll wait two more weeks together."

This is powerful friendship! Lynette's friend didn't offer her an answer or a fix. Instead, she offered to be with Lynette in that space. She had faith that the Lord would strengthen Lynette within that time and bring hope, perspective, and change. He would bring a renewed strength to continue on.

And he did.

Remember that idea of *qavah*? We not only wait with expectation. We bind ourselves together with God. We wait with him. We sit in the sling that holds us close to his chest, and *we hold on*.

This story ministered to me deeply when Lynette shared it. So I sit here with you today, wanting to be for you what Lynette has been to me, and what her friend has been to her. That hard story you're holding, waiting on? Let's wait on the Lord together for two more weeks.

Social Dallas pastor Robert Madu, who I'm honored to also call my brother-in-law, said something in a sermon awhile back that has never left me: "Often, when our experience doesn't line up with our expectation, God is trying to give us a revelation of who he is." Meaning God is trying to reveal something deeper to us about his character, his power, his nature. In seasons of waiting, when we keep saying, "I thought this would be accomplished by now!" the exercise of waiting is less about what we are waiting on and more about knowing God better.

"Wait-y" seasons can be weighty seasons. They are anything but easy. Our souls need to be anchored to truth—especially the truth that God is good, that he knows us, that he desires what is best for us. When we drift away from these truths, our theology will suffer because our heart

is in pain. But when we trust God's power to work within us, we can see his sovereignty as protective. We can say, "Not my will, Lord, but yours be done." We might even be able to see how the wait is preparing us for greater things to come.

Now when I sit in these waiting spaces, I view them as invitations from the Lord to know him in a new way. Instead of praying, "God, why isn't this happening now?" I've started praying, "God, what do you want me to learn about you?"

Everybody is waiting on something. All of us, I think, are waiting to see God's power displayed. Will you know that power when you see it? If you don't know God well, could you miss it? At the end of the day, the real answer to our wait, the answer to all our questions, is *more of God*. This is the truly abundant life. The apostle John said, "Beloved, I pray that you may prosper in all things and be in health, just as your soul prospers" (3 John 1:2 NKJV). Yes, he prayed for the church to prosper, but his number-one desire was the prospering of the people's souls. What we choose to do in the waiting seasons of our lives determines what is produced in us. In our times of trouble, we can develop maturity, endurance, and trust in the Lord, and we can learn more about who he is to us in our deepest needs.

So trust that your waiting season is producing more fruit in your life, which is only the best for you. If you get the answer you think you want, then great—but the real treasure is becoming closer to God through it all.

I am in the middle of a hard day.

Someone in my family is facing something critical and multilayered and, honestly, devastating. Since the crisis unfolded, I've been taking things one day at a time, but today it's the middle of the morning and I can hardly get out of bed. How much longer will we have to keep paying the high price of this pain? When will we know—fully know—the joy of the Lord and his abundant life?

I know it's possible to move forward in life even while we mourn. We can take baby steps. We can find beauty in the middle of our mess.

A friend of mine who is a counselor told me we humans will always find what we are looking for in our days. Are we looking for the hard, the worrisome, the problems, the lack? We'll always find it. Are we looking for the beautiful, the hopeful, the profound, the blessings? We'll find those too.

Today I don't even know what I'm looking for. I'm so drained. I've been juggling painful phone calls and making hard decisions. Today I need to stay home, be still, and nourish my own soul. I think of David strengthening himself in the Lord when he was distressed (1 Sam. 30:6). So that is what I *decide* to do.

I swing my legs off the bed and put my feet on the floor. In an instant, the weight of reality fills my gut with the waters of dread that threaten to sink me. It almost takes my breath away. But as I toss the covers back and walk out of my bedroom, I decide today is going to be a *good* day because God will be at its center. I will look for him today, and I will start by looking for his beauty.

I turn on my coffeepot, and the delicious smell of the beans fills the kitchen. I turn on some soul-feeding worship music. I let the music soothe me, and I meditate on the lyrics, putting my focus and full attention on who God is rather than on the problems that will require my time and energy today. We humans were made to worship. I sit at my little wooden kitchen table that was gifted to me by a friend. It's nothing special, but it's a table where I've poured out my heart to the Lord. I open my Bible and read from the Psalms.

I do believe we become what we choose to behold. When I look down at my phone all day, doomscrolling, I become anxious and worried. When I focus on problems, I become weighed down, consumed by trouble. But when I behold Christ—his faithfulness, goodness, mercy—I become more like him. More full of hope, joy, peace, and all the beautiful attributes of his Spirit.

I finish with the Psalms and begin to read aloud from Matthew 5. When we don't know how or what to pray, letting Scripture do this for us speaks to the deep places.

Blessed are the poor in spirit, for theirs is the kingdom of
heaven.
Blessed are those who mourn, for they shall be comforted.
Blessed are the meek, for they shall inherit the earth.
Blessed are those who hunger and thirst for righteousness, for
they shall be satisfied.
Blessed are the merciful, for they shall receive mercy.
Blessed are the pure in heart, for they shall see God.
Blessed are the peacemakers, for they shall be called sons of
God. (Matt. 5:3–9)

The truth of God's Word begins to permeate my weighed-down heart. The lie that I am alone in this crisis I'm facing begins to fall away from me, and I remember: God is close to the brokenhearted and saves those who are crushed in spirit (Ps. 34:18). Strength for the day infuses my soul.

I don't have the energy to go out, so I order some fresh groceries to be delivered, and around noon I cook a meal that smells great and nourishes me. I call a few friends that I love and respect, and together we process some of what I'm facing. They speak life and hope into me.

I walk around outside in my yard, turning my face up toward the sun, letting it warm me for a few minutes. I breathe deep. Three years ago I planted a peach tree in my yard, and I decide to check in on it. It started as a tiny twig, and each spring I've watched it in great anticipation of fruit. And each year it has bloomed . . . but no peaches.

This afternoon I walk to my tree and gently pull back a new leaf . . . and see something green hanging off a branch. To my amazement, it's a baby peach! I count—not just one or a handful, but *thirty-five* peaches on their way to maturity. I can't believe my eyes!

But of course I can. I looked for beauty and I found it. Even among the hard today, even among the waiting and the questions and the throbbing pain, God's beauty is present. He is strengthening me, growing me, and teaching me dependence on him and him alone.

RESTORATION PRACTICE

Strengthen Yourself in the Lord While You Wait

God's goodness surrounds us anywhere and everywhere we are. In seasons of joy and abundance, and in seasons of pain and want and waiting. *Find the goodness.* Take some time to do one of two options: (1) Journal about the goodness in your day today. Anything that comes to mind, even the smallest joy(s) you experienced. (2) Go outside and take a walk, noticing goodness anywhere you can find it. Seeking out goodness and joy can change us for the better, and can strengthen our muscles of gratitude in tough times. I pray your heart is open to receiving goodness today.

12

COMING
HOME

You Are Wholly Restored in Jesus

G oing home isn't always easy. At times, it has felt challenging for me. But today I feel grateful and reflective as I sit outside a little coffee shop in my hometown of El Dorado, Arkansas—small-town USA at its finest. It's a beautiful fall day, with the perfect breeze and cool crisp air. My absolute favorite. I love coming back during this season. The oaks display all their golden glory, and the evergreen pines stretch so tall. I used to rollerblade with my friends on these streets. Now I'm sitting here drinking my Americano, feeling nostalgic, chatting with people I haven't seen in so long as they pass by.

This little town is special to me and holds so many tender connections, beautiful and familiar places and faces. I love that about it. Seeing people who have known you your whole life is a gift that brings a sense of comfort.

I didn't always feel this way. Memories of home and all it holds flood my mind. Some good and some really, really hard. But every experience has shaped me. At certain points in my life, especially through the beginning of some of my healing process, it has been hard to come here. Instead of being a place of comfort, it felt like the place that housed some of my greatest hardships. For a while I stayed away as much as I could. I wasn't emotionally capable of sorting through the bad and seeing the good. I didn't—I *couldn't*—see my hometown through the filter I do right now.

Seeing life through a healed lens sure helps. I have learned the truth of the statement "Wherever you go, there you are." To whatever degree

I'm healed or hurting, those parts of me show up, and I can extend them grace and gratitude and love.

Because the story I carry inside myself isn't so much about where I am as who I am becoming.

This state of repair—this state of *becoming*—is where we spend most of our lives. One of the questions I'm asked most frequently these days about the house restoration (which is a go-to conversation starter for a lot of folks) goes like this: "How far along are you on the house? Like on a scale from one to ten, how done are you?"

That's a tough question. For as long as I own this home, I don't think I'll ever be done. I can't imagine a day when I tie a big red bow on the roof and walk outside and yell, "That's it! It's perfect! The house is officially restored!" As much as I've accomplished in my home, I still see things daily I would love to upgrade or improve. As a visionary, I'm constantly walking into rooms and seeing more that I want to do. For instance, I love light, light, and more light! I would just love to replace a certain wall in my dining room with windows and French doors. I could sit at my table, drink my coffee, and get a good view of my little courtyard. I want to add beautiful landscaping and a sprinkler system. The floors are original and really rugged, and while I love the look, they need some TLC to stop deterioration. I want to add a second bathroom because, as I'm sure some of you know, having only one bathroom can sometimes be a challenge.

I am not stretching the truth when I say this house is an ongoing work in progress with no clear end date. There's no end of jobs that need to be done, but that's life. That's a fact I've learned not to resent but to accept. The home is evolving over time. Like me, it is . . . becoming.

That truth used to bother me. Thought patterns of "I will never be finished" and "I can never get this done" drove me to feeling down and stuck. It was when I learned to live in this tension that I began to gain momentum in the restoration of the house. The bones are good. It's set on a good foundation. It's safe and sturdy. I've experienced its beauty.

I've got a good thing going over here! This includes all the lessons that help me to improve, grow, and learn.

And I just want to say, as a recovering perfectionist and people pleaser, being able to write that out represents huge progress in my journey.

Though we might be tempted to think our ultimate objective is some manufactured state of perfection, our most profound experiences with Jesus actually happen along the road to where we're going—which, by the way, will never be perfection. We experience the depths of his love as he tends to our wounds and reveals that our true identity is in him as things are *now*. "Abide in me, and I in you," Jesus told his disciples. "As the branch cannot bear fruit by itself, unless it abides in the vine, neither can you, unless you abide in me. I am the vine; you are the branches. Whoever abides in me and I in him, he it is that bears much fruit, for apart from me you can do nothing" (John 15:4–5). He is with us here and now, wherever that may be, whatever state we're in. If we can trust God's sovereignty and goodness as Job did, we can be filled with faith in him and receive peace during the process.

I've come to think of this well-being as the shalom of my life. The noun *shalom* is derived from the verbal root *shalam*, which means "to restore." Psalm 34:14 in the Passion Translation reads, "Make 'peace' your life motto." A footnote to the word *peace* tells us:

> Twice in this verse David used the Hebrew word *shalom*. This word means much more than "peace." It means wholeness, wellness, well-being, safe, happy, friendly, favor, completeness, to make peace, peace offering, secure, to prosper, to be victorious, to be content, tranquil, quiet, and restful. So *shalom* is used to describe those of us who have been provided all that is needed to be whole and complete and break off all authority that would attempt to bind us to chaos.[1]

Read that again: We have been "provided all that is needed to be whole and complete and break off all authority that would attempt to bind us to chaos." Thank the Lord peace doesn't have to wait for perfection! We only have to agree that God has the power to end our relationship with chaos. What a gift.

Your life and mine are happening now. If we wait on perfection before stepping into God's purposes for us, we'll be waiting until heaven. We don't have to do that. Look at all the imperfect people Jesus called into purpose during his time on earth. If we wait around for perfect circumstances or total healing before we feel qualified or worthy or whole enough to step into his purposes for us, we will never step in. Ecclesiastes 11:4–5 says, "Farmers who wait for perfect weather never plant. If they watch every cloud, they never harvest. Just as you cannot understand the path of the wind or the mystery of a tiny baby growing in its mother's womb, so you cannot understand the activity of God, who does all things" (NLT).

Sometimes we have to move as we mourn. Certain things are going to feel undone and unfinished this side of heaven because we are human, but we can still press on and progress. So much of this world is a mystery. We are called to move forward in faith and to trust that God will do what we cannot in a way that is beyond our understanding (see Eph. 3:20).

So plant your seeds. What is God calling you to do in the shalom of your life?

In the past, when I would reflect on my life, I never thought, "I should write a book about that someday." That thought never occurred to me until a literary agent approached me with the idea. Even now, I don't think about my life in terms of it being a great story. It's simply the story I have lived and continue to live. I came to this project far from any finish line of calling my life—or my house—fully restored. But I felt called by God to do it. I jumped into the ocean as a person who couldn't swim, and some days I felt like I was drowning.

My good friend Christy Nockels encouraged me one day when I was doubting my ability to write this message. She texted:

Hey, you CAN do this! But it might be one of
the hardest things ever. You're gonna have to
give yourself loads of grace while also pushing
yourself beyond your limits! You have been
through some REALLY hard things in your life
and God has made you into a resilient and wise
woman! You've got what it takes because HE'S IN
YOU but it's gonna feel like climbing Mt. Everest.
If you've ever watched anything on people who
have climbed Everest, they have to do SO much
training (which you've done!) but then they have
to take that training and begin to acclimate to
the environment by climbing and descending and
doing that over and over until they reach the top.
This is where you are in the journey . . . you're
acclimating. You're going up and coming back
down, going up, coming back down . . . and then
. . . you'll eventually reach the top. But as you
might know, when people get to the top, they can
only stay about 10 minutes (tops!) when they
REACH the summit or they'll die. And then they
quickly descend. Just keep "acclimating" each
day. Go up and come back down. Push really hard
and then go back down and hide and rest. You'll
eventually reach the summit. You will.

She was right. I eventually got there, and now you hold this book in
your hands. But even there, standing on the peak and feeling the rush
of the accomplishment (I wrote a *book*!), we look out over the vistas of
our lives and what do we see? Many more mountains to climb. "I've
done *this*, and now I need to do *that*." This side of heaven, we're never
truly done.

Does that thought exhaust you? Philippians 1 contains a promise
that keeps me going. Paul is addressing the church in Philippi, which
means he is talking to believers in Jesus. He starts out by exhorting them
and telling them he is thankful to the Lord as he remembers them and
thinks of their partnership in the gospel. He then goes on to speak hope
and encouragement to them, reminding them, "I am sure of this, that he
who began a good work in you will bring it to completion at the day of

Jesus Christ" (v. 6). Christ himself will complete the good work he has started in me! The pressure is not on me but on him.

The One who is with me.

The One who loves me.

The One who heals the brokenhearted.

The One who is all-powerful and holy.

I do what I can do, then Christ in me does what I could *never* do. So many days I need this reminder.

We often have to fight a production mentality, which is the lie that we carry the weight of the world on our own shoulders and have to make everything happen on our own. I'm learning that this work of completion only comes through daily surrender and partnership with God—a conscious laying down of my life in exchange for Christ's power and strength. When I equate abiding with producing or with carrying the load myself, I end up exhausted, burned-out, and frustrated. But according to John 15, our role is to abide in the Vine (that is, Christ). Apart from him we can do nothing. He will produce. I don't know about you, but I've tended to overcomplicate this. Exhaustion, burnout, and frustration are not required on this journey.

When we're in that deep chasm between where we are and where we long to be, the grace of God abounds and does its best work.

When we're in that deep chasm between where we are and where we long to be, the grace of God abounds and does its best work. Some things are simply too big for us, too heavy for our shoulders, and way beyond our capabilities. *And that's okay.* Writer and speaker Bob Goff likes to say, "We're all rough drafts of the people we are still becoming." (After writing this book I have a deeper appreciation for his metaphor.) We keep on writing and assessing and revising as we go, getting better every day. Because of Christ's mercy, we have confidence in his sovereignty. He really is making all things new.

At the café in El Dorado, I finish my Americano and wave goodbye to someone I know from years back. I climb into my car and leave the coffee shop, then decide to take a meandering drive around town before heading to a relative's house for a visit. I drive by the sites of so many memories—my old high school, restaurants I used to frequent, the "avenue" my friends and I would cruise up and down all hours of the night. It's easier to be here now than it used to be, and I think it would be a good time to tip my hat to the childhood home where so many hard times had come to pass. After all, so many good times happened there too.

I turn the car onto my old street and drive slowly past the small houses with their painted wooden siding and brick-covered foundations. I remember each one. How many times did my siblings and our friends *fly* down that sidewalk on our bikes and—

I slowly approach the lot of our old home. I *don't* remember this. How could I? I've never seen it. I hit the brakes, and when my shock wears off, I pull the car to the curb.

The house of my childhood has been bulldozed, razed, and hauled away.

Not a scrap remains, nothing but four towering trees and the low wall that divided our driveway from our neighbor's.

Grass is growing where the house used to be. Green is taking over. New shoots of life.

My dream is becoming a reality.

After signing the papers and buying my farmhouse in 2018, I wished everything could be a breeze. I'd proclaimed the word *restoration* like a banner over my home and life on my social media platforms. I'd begun sharing my story and celebrating the progress, documenting it with photos. I'd begun to speak from my heart, telling the story of the home and how the Lord was also restoring me. But a year into home ownership, I continued to battle the two hellish monsters of anxiety and depression on and off. I was physically tired from the labor and emotionally tired after asking so long for the Lord to heal me fully. I felt spiritually worn-out and worried I was losing my footing again.

I can promise you some tough days during your process of being restored. Some days will be a fight. Some mornings it will take everything you have to get up, put on the armor of God, choose to think good thoughts, and believe God's Word. The journey to healing is hard and holy work. But I can also promise you that God will keep showing up. With him, you can dare to dream.

I never used to dream with God. There were too many rules and risks in my head. But over the past few years I've learned how much he delights in my dreams and that I can trust him with my hopes and desires. I can trust him with . . . me. My trust in him, my anticipation of his good gifts, and my hope in all the things he can do that are yet to be accomplished have freed me.

Lately, instead of being so immersed in the story of my life, I am able to speak about this healing season from a different place. A strengthened place. I am speaking "*into* it" from the safety and security of God's love rather than "*from* it" as a wounded and lonely soul. It has been a slow and dynamic process of redeeming pain. Now I see that the wounds were not fatal, nor were they a prison that could hold me forever.

The journey to healing is hard and holy work.

Few things in this life are permanent, least of all a permanent residence in suffering. God wants to love us back to life. We only have to receive it from him.

Recently someone asked me, "Do you think you'll live in the house forever?"

The first time I pondered that question, I wasn't sure. Look at what I've invested in this place. How could I even consider leaving? But this time the question landed differently. I sensed something in me had shifted, but I'd been unaware. I stood in the kitchen and slowly nodded, thinking through my answer. Looking back at them I said, "You know, I don't really know what will come of this house, but I feel my heart shifting a bit. I've been immersed in this season, heart and soul. From the beginning of my life to the purchase of the home, I've been living this story of restoration. I'm walking these floors, restoring these rooms, putting my hands to the plow. But it's not just about the house. It's

spiritual, physical, emotional. It's about my whole being *living restored*."
I was thinking of the apostle Paul referring to us as living epistles: "You are our epistle written in our hearts, known and read by all men; clearly you are an epistle of Christ, ministered by us, written not with ink but by the Spirit of the living God, not on tablets of stone but on tablets of flesh, that is, of the heart" (2 Cor. 3:2–3 NKJV).

I can rest in the promise that whatever the future holds, with Christ, it is well with my soul.

I'm unsure exactly what the Lord has next for me. Will I keep the house forever and live somewhere else? Will I stay here and continue to evolve with it? Will it become a home for others? I don't know, but I don't need to have all the answers to these questions.

I can rest in the promise that whatever the future holds, with Christ, it is well with my soul.

I stood at my kitchen sink one morning recently, staring out the window while talking to a friend on the phone. She was sharing with me about a heartache in her life and time lost with a parent. Because of challenges her family faced, including mental illness and addiction, she was grieving the loss of the kind of parenting she had longed for but never received. Instead she had to be a parental figure to herself. This caused pain and complicated her life in distressing ways.

Deep empathy for her led me to tell her about a passage in Joel I had just read.

> I will restore to you the years
>   that the swarming locust has eaten,
> the hopper, the destroyer, and the cutter,
>   my great army, which I sent among you.
>
> You shall eat in plenty and be satisfied,
>   and praise the name of the LORD your God,
>   who has dealt wondrously with you.
> And my people shall never again be put to shame. (2:25–26)

Something hit me fresh when I read this familiar passage: The Lord won't only restore our tangible losses; he will also restore lost time. Many of us grieve the lost years we would have spent with a loved one or doing something important. God sees, and God cares. Humans can restore some things—they can give back money or property, for example. But only God can restore time. Only a God who stands outside of time can give it back to us and make it richer, better, fuller. I don't know how he does it, but I know it to be true. I have experienced it. This passage offers us restoration hope that the time ravaged by hardships and pain is never wasted. It will be redeemed and filled with blessings in God's timing and in his way.

Shame is one of the battles of the mind that robbed me of so many years. It started when my parents divorced. Because we lived in a small town and they were in ministry, it felt very public. A bit later, when I experienced other trauma, the hurt deepened. I isolated myself physically and emotionally. I made a home for myself in that shame space. I walked everywhere and did everything while carrying the weight of it. I didn't know life without it.

Then I began to walk in God's promises and to experience the freedom and joy of being known and loved and chosen by him. In Isaiah 61:7 he promises, "Instead of your shame there shall be a double portion; instead of dishonor they shall rejoice in their lot; therefore in their land they shall possess a double portion; they shall have everlasting joy." Over the years, the Lord has made a divine reversal of my shame. I stand tall in my identity in Christ, who has brought me a double portion of joy and honor. He has given me a gift of photography that has taken me into the homes of influential people and made room for me at tables in high places (Prov. 18:16). Only God could replace so much heartache, abandonment, and shame with such a blessing.

Tonight I'm coming home. Not to my childhood hometown or to the home that was bulldozed, but to my little farmhouse. It has come to represent much more to me than I ever could have imagined.

I deplane at DFW and fetch my luggage. I haul my equipment to my car and load it up, then slide into the driver's seat and take just a minute to let my body sink into something comfortable, familiar. Returning from a distant place is less exciting in some ways than the thrill of the adventure, but nothing beats the feeling of returning to a place that offers safety and peace.

As I navigate the airport exits and pull onto the familiar highway, I think about someone else's return home—that young man we call the prodigal from Jesus's story in Luke 15. Recently, I heard a pastor say he wished we didn't call this "The Parable of the Prodigal Son." I was sitting in the congregation and wondered why he thought that. I leaned in. "If I'd been the one deciding how to subtitle these stories in the Bible," he said, "I would have named it 'The Love of the Father.'" He then called our attention to the prodigal's homecoming. The young man was returning despondent and ashamed, ruined by life.

> But while he was still a long way off, his father saw him and felt compassion, and ran and embraced him and kissed him. And the son said to him, "Father, I have sinned against heaven and before you. I am no longer worthy to be called your son." But the father said to his servants, "Bring quickly the best robe, and put it on him, and put a ring on his hand, and shoes on his feet. And bring the fattened calf and kill it, and let us eat and celebrate. For this my son was dead, and is alive again; he was lost, and is found." And they began to celebrate. (vv. 20–24)

Looking at the parable through that lens, I can see it's all about the father's love. I think about the joy that dad must have felt when he saw his son coming down the road, coming back home where his shame could have no power over him. That boy made some choices that most of us would feel ashamed of, but his father didn't hold that history against him. Imagine the father's compassion also overflowing to a child returning home after being battered by life through no fault of his own. Is there any greater love?

If I weren't driving, I'd close my eyes and soak up the thought of the forgiveness, compassion, and extravagant love of the father meeting the son right where he was. Everything else I've been taught about this story pales in comparison to this truth—that no matter what path we have traveled through life, our Father is always waiting for us to come home. When we do, he rushes to meet us and pours out his perfect love all over us. He rejoices over us, celebrates us, puts a robe of righteousness on us.

In our seasons of healing, the enemy of our souls will want us to believe we don't deserve restoration. He will whisper in our ear, "You can't go back home." He will try to bombard our minds with shame and memories of things we have done, things that have been done to us, how broken we are. That is *not* the heart of the Father. The central theme of the gospel is "come as you are." God will work in our lives. He will do the mending and the repairing. We must anchor ourselves in the truth that he loves us more than we can comprehend.

He just wants us to come home.

I take the highway exit just as the sun drops below the horizon, and my car's headlights pop on automatically, illuminating the dusky road. I make a quick stop to collect my precious pup, Belle, from the people who care for her while I'm away. She's excited to see me and climbs into the car, eager to head back to our place.

As the sky darkens, I don't worry about the sparsely lit streets that lead into my neighborhood. This place has become so familiar to me that I might be able to get home blindfolded. My yearning eases up a bit. I'm close. We're almost there.

I think about my friend who has lost years and dreams to the locusts of a pained childhood. If I said to her, "God just wants you home," what is meant to be a promise might feel like a knife in the gut. What is home, after all? For her, it was a place of grief and disappointment, a place that couldn't be trusted, that might not be safe or stable. When she hears people talk about home, her yearning for the dream of what home could be is so deep that tears come to her eyes. The dream seems

too far out of reach. I remember feeling that way once. I want to help her carry the load of pain.

It took a long time and a lot of God's patience for me to realize that my true home is not this little farmhouse. Though God has given me a physical home and healed me from my old heartache, I know this is not what I've been seeking. In my spiritual life, I understand that true restoration leads me to Jesus.

Jesus is our home, and this home will never go away. All the yearnings we have ever had are satisfied in him. No matter what the earthly "home" of our physical lives might look like, we always have a perfect spiritual home in him. We can be with him, and others can be with us, in this real, eternal home even while we are still in restoration season here on earth.

Belle and I pull up in front of the house. It's so very different from the day I first laid eyes on it with Meredith. So much of the "beyond" that the Lord granted me to see then is a reality now, right down to the porch swing and the little bird box where a mama bluebird has made her own home and sits on her eggs.

I slip my key into the doorknob, turn it, and the door glides open in welcome. Belle rushes in for a drink of water, and I let my bags slide off my shoulders. I'm welcomed with the scent of my favorite laundry soap and the fresh Texas air from a kitchen window I left cracked open. I pick up my favorite quilt that has slipped off the sofa and turn on a table lamp. The gold light spills over the floor, and I hear the sounds of home.

I eat a good dinner and decide the dishes can wait until tomorrow. I turn down the bed, then slip into lavender-salt bathwater and wash all the travel away. Tonight, my thoughts are not on all the undone work and the never-ending projects, or the doubts that I am up to any of the tasks that await me tomorrow. Tonight I am overflowing with gratitude for the Father's compassionate love. He has leveled the ruins of my life and erected beauty in its place. He has strengthened me with his love and restored my lost hope.

For now, I am content to soak in his love.

There is hope beyond your pain, beyond the brokenness. Partner with God in the restoration story he wants to tell in your life. The work will feel impossible some days, but he has all the expertise you need to rely on. Allow Jesus to replace your ineffective efforts with foundational, lasting transformation. Invite the Holy Spirit to shine light on these truths about your life: You are loved. You are priceless. You are worthy of repair.

The true healing your soul craves awaits you. Through Jesus you can experience abundance of soul. You can know shalom—nothing missing, nothing broken. He is faithful to complete what he starts in you, and he will never abandon you. All he asks of you is your willingness. Your surrender. Lean in and trust his power in you.

And while our becoming and our healing are always in-process here on earth, remember that in Christ alone, you are already fully and wholly restored.

You are loved beyond what you can imagine. And I am here, friend, cheering you on as you are becoming and as you discover the profound joy of your own restoration journey.

RESTORATION PRACTICE

Make Way for the Shalom of Your Life

As children of God, we have access to his peace, which transcends our own understanding. The shalom of God is not easily explained by human logic. In Philippians 4:4–8, the apostle Paul lays out the actions we can take as we tap into this supernatural peace. Here's my own paraphrase of his words:

> Always be full of joy in the Lord.
> I say it again—REJOICE in the Lord!
> Let everyone see that you are considerate in all you do.
> REMEMBER, the Lord is coming again soon!
> Don't worry about anything; instead, PRAY about everything.
> FIX YOUR MIND on what is true.
> PRACTICE these things.
> Tell God what you need and THANK him for what he has already done!
> This is a way to experience God's peace, which will guard your heart and mind.

RESTORATION PROMISES

The LORD is my shepherd; I shall not want.
   He makes me lie down in green pastures.
He leads me beside still waters.
   He restores my soul. (Ps. 23:1–3)

The LORD upholds all who are falling
   and raises up all who are bowed down. (Ps. 145:14)

He gives power to the faint,
   and to him who has no might he increases strength.
Even youths shall faint and be weary,
   and young men shall fall exhausted;
but they who wait for the LORD shall renew their strength;
   they shall mount up with wings like eagles;
they shall run and not be weary;
   they shall walk and not faint. (Isa. 40:29–31)

Instead of your shame there shall be a double portion;
   instead of dishonor they shall rejoice in their lot;
therefore in their land they shall possess a double portion;
   they shall have everlasting joy. (Isa. 61:7)

I will give them a heart to know that I am the LORD, and they shall be my people and I will be their God, for they shall return to me with their whole heart. (Jer. 24:7)

For I know the plans I have for you, declares the LORD, plans for welfare and not for evil, to give you a future and a hope. (Jer. 29:11)

And I will give you a new heart, and a new spirit I will put within you. And I will remove the heart of stone from your flesh and give you a heart of flesh. (Ezek. 36:26)

I will restore to you the years that the swarming locust has eaten. (Joel 2:25)

Come to me, all who labor and are heavy laden, and I will give you rest. (Matt. 11:28)

The thief comes only to steal and kill and destroy. I came that they may have life and have it abundantly. (John 10:10)

Do not be conformed to this world, but be transformed by the renewal of your mind, that by testing you may discern what is the will of God, what is good and acceptable and perfect. (Rom. 12:2)

Therefore, if anyone is in Christ, he is a new creation. The old has passed away; behold, the new has come. (2 Cor. 5:17)

And I am sure of this, that he who began a good work in you will bring it to completion at the day of Jesus Christ. (Phil. 1:6)

It is God who works in you, both to will and to work for his good pleasure. (Phil. 2:13)

ACKNOWLEDGMENTS

To my great God and the Master Restorer, Jesus Christ, the One who mends the brokenhearted and has taken the ashes of my life and brought beauty. I am grateful to you for loving me, dying for me, and giving me abundant life. You are good and faithful forever. You make all things new! All glory and honor belong to you. This book is yours, Jesus.

So many people have supported and encouraged me as I wrote this book.

Dad, I love you. I have watched you champion people in restoration since as early as I can remember. I have learned so much from you. Thank you for cheering me on in God's call on my life. I can still hear your voice yelling from the stands at my games, "Go, Meshali! Go!" That echoes in my head today. Thank you for supporting me and believing in me always. I love you and honor you, Dad.

Tracey, God expanded and added to my life when we became family. You have always been a cheerleader and made me feel exceptional at anything I put my hands to. You'll never know how much I appreciate that. You were always telling me, "Your book's going to be amazing! You can do this!" Those words carried further than you know! Your personal story of resilience and restoration has inspired me. I love you, T!

Mom, I often tell people that I get my love for all things creative from you—including my love for photography. You taught me from a young age to see beyond and look for potential and beauty even in the unwanted things. I saw you do that with houses, rooms, and furniture growing up. Thank you for supporting this book and telling me to share openly and honestly. That brought my heart freedom to do so. I love and honor you, Mom.

Taylor Madu—my sister, my best friend—our stories and our hearts are intertwined, and I'm forever grateful for the bond we share. From the first page to now, you have always been there for me. Thank you for continually cheering me on and reminding me of God's power to heal and restore. We have lived out so much of that together! I can always hear you in my head saying, "There's purpose in this! This is going to change the world!" God is faithful. You are a trophy of God's restoration! I love you more than words can say.

Trey Mitchell, I'm so grateful you are my brother. I am thankful for our relationship and that as we've walked together in the best and hardest of times, we have always had each other. You have encouraged me and made me feel like I could do anything! Thank you for that. I love you forever, bud.

Hunter Orcutt, being your sister is such an honor and a joy! When God brought you into my life at such a young age, he expanded my life and my heart. He knew we needed each other. I remember the first time I ever saw you and held you. Your story of restoration has inspired me. I love you, Nunner!

Kristi Elia, you have always been so much more than an aunt to me. You've always stood as a pillar, and still do! It is not lost on me the deep love and sacrifice you have poured into my life. From the time I was little, cruising around in your red Probe and going to your cheerleading practices, I have looked up to you and am so grateful for the time you have invested into my life. You have helped shape who I have become. I love you.

Elaine Mitchell, thank you for believing in me. Having you as a grandmother is such a gift, and I'm deeply grateful for you. We have a coffee date on the schedule soon. Meet me at the kitchen table! I love you, Mimi!

Peggy McDaniel, I'm in awe of what the Lord has done! Wow, what a journey it's been! The first day I reluctantly walked into your office and sat at that little wooden desk, you looked me in the eyes and saw past a lot of pain, and you called out the greatness. Thank you for that. You have been "Jesus with skin on" to me. Your unconditional love, unwavering support, and steady encouragement in my journey have been a key in God transforming me. He truly does make our place of weeping a place of springs, as you assured me he would (Ps. 84:6). He is faithful. Love heals.

Pastor Rhonda Davis, only heaven will tell the amazing ways you have impacted me. You reminded me long ago that God is faithful and would indeed establish me and heal my heart in the deep places. He has done just that. Roots and wings. You have taught me so much about restoration, ministry, and never being beyond God's reach. Your heart for the "whosoever" has inspired me beyond words. You live this message out with boots on the ground. You have gotten in the trenches with me, and I am forever thankful God gave me you. I love you deeply!

Steve and Susan Blount, I don't believe this book would have been written without you. I truly don't. You saw a book in me and believed in me long (long!) before I ever saw a book in myself. From phone calls to Zoom calls to visits at the house over carrot cake, you never stopped encouraging me. You have always looked out for me. I see it. Your friendship is a great gift. I love you!

Mike Salisbury and the team at Yates and Yates, you are incredible! Thank you for championing this message of *Restored*. You guys have walked me through the process from day one. I deeply appreciate you. Mike, in our first meeting, you spoke so much life into me and saw a book in me before I did. You have been patient with me as I have actually lived out this message and allowed God to "work it out in me." Now it's words on a page—"Hey, I wrote a book! Yay!" Thanks for walking alongside me and seeing it all the way to the finish line.

Leah Ost, you are a true and faithful friend. Your love and support in my writing process and stepping into my calling have encouraged my heart to be brave. Thank you for taking that plane ride and coming to visit me during a hard time. That's one of countless ways you have been a great friend. It marked me and is now an example for many of a great kingdom friendship. Grateful we are family! All in for all time!

Christy Nockels, your voice has been so pivotal in my life, and your encouragement in my book journey has given me wings. Thank you for your love, support, and guidance. Your door at Keepers Branch has always been open for me . . . to write and dream or just be. From day one you've carved out a place for me in your heart and in your home. You are a big sister to me. Your friendship is a blessing in my life. I love you.

Pastors Stephen and Thelisa Nutt, you are two of the greatest people and pastors I know. Thank you for your investment in my life, starting all those years ago. Pastor Stephen, thank you for encouraging me to buy this house, even when I felt scared. You told me I had to step out of the boat to walk on water. Thelisa, thank you for stopping by my office and inviting me to have lunch and go for Sonic runs, and for loving me during my college years. Thank you for being intentional. God really began some deep heart work in me around that time. Y'all are an inspiration and have impacted my life greatly. Love you both!

Andrea Howey, thank you for being a faithful friend in this journey. From that first day I went to look at the farmhouse, you have "seen beyond" with me. The number of times we've sat at the farmhouse and dreamed over coffee or queso is more than I can count. All the talks and prayers have spurred me on in the good and in the harder days. What a gift you are. I love you, friend!

Toni Comiskey, God connected our hearts in his perfect timing, and what an encouragement you have been to me in my life and during this writing process. Thank you for your friendship and for every visit, for every phone call . . . and for always listening when I call you back with "one more thing." I love you!

Erin Healy, working alongside you has been an absolute dream. Your gifting, professionalism, and empathy (and the list goes on) have taken this project to the next level. Thank you for mapping out this idea with me and helping bring it to life.

Scotti Beth Lawson, having you on my team is such a gift! Thank you for being an amazing assistant and friend—for holding my arms up on days I was feeling spread thin. Your prayers have helped carry this project into fruition. I am so grateful for you. Love you!

To the amazing team at Revell, including but not limited to Kelsey Bowen, Amy Nemecek, Nadine Rewa, Laura Klynstra, and Eileen Hanson: I am absolutely blown away by you all! You have helped me bring this book to life and made the process enjoyable. Thank you for your hard work, care, and the great attention to detail you poured into the whole project from start to finish. I am forever grateful!

NOTES

Foreword

1. Trevor Persaud, "Chilean Miner: 'God Has Never Left Us,'" *Christianity Today*, October 12, 2010, https://www.christianitytoday.com/news/2010/october/chilean-miner-god-has-never-left-us.html.

2. Dallas Baptist University, "Chilean Miner Speaks in Chapel," *DBU Report* (Winter 2012–2013), 16.

Chapter 1 Paradise Lost

1. Graham Joseph Hill, "How to Write a Lament," *Graham Joseph Hill* (blog), December 15, 2023, https://grahamjosephhill.com/lament/.

Chapter 2 Every Heart but Mine

1. A. W. Tozer, *Knowledge of the Holy* (1961; repr., Victoria, BC: Reading Essentials, n.d.), loc. 43 of 1805, Kindle.

2. "Gethsemane Definition," That the World May Know with Ray Vander Laan, accessed July 8, 2024, https://www.thattheworldmayknow.com/define-gethsemane.

3. N. T. Wright, *Lent for Everyone: Matthew Year A* (London: SPCK, 2011), 126.

Chapter 3 The House God Sees

1. Lauren Slater, "Black Swans," *The Missouri Review* 19, no. 1 (1996): 29, https://doi.org/10.1353/mis.1996.0015.

2. C. S. Lewis, *Mere Christianity* (New York: Macmillan, 1960), 160. Copyright © 1942, 1943, 1944, 1952 C. S. Lewis Pte. Ltd. Extract reprinted by permission.

Chapter 6 The Apprentice

1. *The New Strong's Expanded Exhaustive Concordance of the Bible*, s.v. "*qavah*" (Nashville: Thomas Nelson, 2010).

Chapter 8 The Load-Bearing Beams of Soul Care

1. John Ortberg, *Soul Keeping: Caring for the Most Important Part of You* (Grand Rapids: Zondervan, 2014), 39.
2. Dan B. Allender and Tremper Longman III, *The Cry of the Soul: How Our Emotions Reveal Our Deepest Questions about God* (Dallas: Word, 1994), 24–25, quoted in Peter Scazzero, *Emotionally Healthy Spirituality* (Grand Rapids: Zondervan, 2017), 73–74.
3. Aria Bendix, "Writing by Hand May Increase Brain Connectivity More Than Typing, Readings of Student Brains Suggest," NBC News, January 27, 2024, https://www.nbcnews.com/health/health-news/writing-by-hand-may-increase-brain-connectivity-rcna135880.
4. Parker J. Palmer, *Let Your Life Speak: Listening for the Voice of Vocation* (San Francisco: Jossey-Bass, 2000), 30–31, quoted in Scazzero, *Emotionally Healthy Spirituality*, 35.

Chapter 9 The Pillars of Purpose

1. Katherine Wolf, "Who We Are," Hope Heals, https://hopeheals.com/who-we-are.
2. Wikipedia, s.v. "Phil Robertson," last modified April 8, 2024, https://en.wikipedia.org/wiki/Phil_Robertson.
3. Rebecca Bender, *In Pursuit of Love: One Woman's Journey from Trafficked to Triumphant* (Grand Rapids: Zondervan, 2020).

Chapter 10 The Buttress of Community

1. Ann Voskamp's Facebook page, accessed July 24, 2024, https://www.facebook.com/AnnVoskamp/photos/maybe-on-the-days-we-want-out-of-our-lives-it-isnt-so-much-that-we-want-to-die-f/1497686953576807/.
2. Edward T. Welch, *A Small Book About Why We Hide: How Jesus Rescues Us from Insecurity, Regret, Failure, and Shame* (Greensboro: New Growth Press, 2021), 5.

Chapter 11 Waiting in the Mess

1. Dave Ramsey, *The Total Money Makeover: A Proven Plan for Financial Fitness* (Nashville: Thomas Nelson, 2013), 29.
2. Anne Lamott, "Anne Lamott Shares All That She Knows: 'Everyone Is Screwed Up, Broken, Clingy, and Scared,'" *Salon*, April 10, 2015, https://www.salon.com/2015/04/10/anne_lamott_shares_all_that_she_knows_everyone_is_screwed_up_broken_clingy_and_scared/.

Chapter 12 Coming Home

1. The Passion Translation® is a registered trademark of Passion & Fire Ministries, Inc. Copyright © 2020 Passion & Fire Ministries, Inc.

Meshali Mitchell is an Arkansas native, Texas resident, and frequent world traveler—a portrait artist, lover of people, and storyteller. The quality of her work stands alone, known by its immersion in heart and soul. She is the owner and operator of Meshali Mitchell, LLC, which is run out of her home but takes her all over the world. She is a creative image builder, confident in her style, and recognized for her ability to capture the true heart of a moment. She believes every human being has a story worth hearing and a story worth telling.

Connect with Meshali:

www.meshali.co

 @meshalimitchellco

@meshali

@meshali